ROLL UP YOUR SLEEVES

ROLL
UP YOUR
SLEEVES

*Leading and Living
in a World of
Constant Change*

MICHAEL ALAN TATE

NEW YORK

LONDON • NASHVILLE • MELBOURNE • VANCOUVER

Roll Up Your Sleeves

Leading and Living in a World of Constant Change

Published in New York, New York, by Morgan James Publishing. Morgan James is a trademark of Morgan James, LLC. www.MorganJamesPublishing.com

ISBN 9781642799767 paperback
ISBN 9781642799774 eBook
Library of Congress Control Number: 2019958031

Cover & Interior Design by:
Christopher Kirk
www.GFSstudio.com

Editorial assistance by:
Minnie Lamberth

Morgan James is a proud partner of Habitat for Humanity Peninsula and Greater Williamsburg. Partners in building since 2006.

Get involved today! Visit
MorganJamesPublishing.com/giving-back

Professional Dedication

*This book was written as an attempt to reflect the wisdom of authors William Bridges and Susan Bridges. The deep thinking and practical application in their magnificent book **Managing Transitions** makes it a must-read for anyone who desires to learn how to lead and live well in this world of constant change.*

Personal Dedication

To my sister Gloria who, when blindsided by a surgery gone terribly wrong, faced her new truth with undaunted courage and continues to stride forward grace upon grace.

We resist transition, not because we can't accept the change, but because we can't accept letting go of that piece of ourselves that we have to give up, when and because, the situation has changed. – William Bridges

Life is difficult. This is a great truth, one of the greatest truths. It is a great truth because once we truly see this truth, we transcend it. Once we truly know that life is difficult—once we truly understand and accept it—then life is no longer difficult. Because once it is accepted, the fact that life is difficult no longer matters. – M. Scott Peck, M.D.

But they that wait upon the Lord shall renew their strength; they shall mount up with wings as eagles; they shall run, and not be weary; and they shall walk, and not faint. – Isaiah 40:31, KJV

TABLE OF CONTENTS

INTRODUCTION

My cell phone rang. I pulled off the road and heard a voice in distress.

On that bright Monday afternoon, I was driving to a hotel located near my client's place of business. My plan was to arrive early, have a relaxing evening, and start fresh to work with the leaders of this organization the next day.

The voice on the phone was the CEO. "A tragic death happened this weekend," she said. "The child of one of our long-time employees was killed in a traffic accident. Almost everyone here knew the teenager and people are really shaken up. We are concerned about this family's loss, but also about the safety of our people as they deal with the impact of this loss at work. Many employees are worried about what they need to do or say or not say when the parent comes back to work. So, Mike, since you are going to be with us tomorrow, would you mind talking with the group about how to handle this?"

"I will," I said. Then I thought, "How will I do this?" The issue was a serious one that deserved more than I could offer off the cuff. Instead of Googling "ways to handle grief and loss," I said a prayer. Then I called a few friends and colleagues whom I knew had experienced this type of loss personally and dealt with it professionally. I received sage advice that helped me prepare for my meeting with the employee group the next morning.

When I arrived, there were twenty or so employees in the room. I explained to them that I was not a licensed psychologist, a grief counselor, or a pastor. Then I asked the group three questions: *Have you ever experienced a tragic loss in your life? Do you recall anything that someone did or said that was helpful? What was not so helpful?*

They shared several helpful ideas and not so helpful ideas, and we processed their insights as a group. Some were still struggling and would have a hard time for a while. Still, a shift in outlook began as, one by one, many of the people in the room realized they knew what to do or not to do, but had just forgotten because of their state of shock.

Loss happens to all of us and causes us to have to face change. Sometimes change is the happy kind; other times it's the grief that hits deep. Yet there is always a way to process the change and move forward.

Unless you live alone on an off-the-map desert island, you will probably experience: the loss of a friendship or the start of a new one, marriage, divorce, separation, the birth of a child, a serious illness, financial problems, or the death of someone close to you.

If you are employed, your organization has been or will soon be affected by reorganization or restructuring due to a merger, acquisition, technology change, leadership change, or just going out of business altogether. The effects could range from a job loss, a new job, a demotion, promotion, relocation, or managing of the employees who remain.

Change is constant. How you respond to change is about the emotional and behavioral choices you make. This book is about choosing a better way to adjust to change yourself and then learning how to help others adjust in a healthy way when change rattles their world.

As I mentioned to my client's team, I am not a licensed psychologist or an educated theologian. I am simply a management consultant, father, grandfather, brother, and spouse who has learned from some very smart people, and also observed certain patterns over decades of working with leaders and employees and living with family members as they experienced both personal and organizational change.

Rather than taking a clinical approach to managing change and coping with stress, I'm offering more of a collection of common-sense approaches that may be helpful to you in your leadership and in your personal life. I'm doing so in a parable because parables are more fun to write (and I hope more fun to read) than instructional manuals. Also, I have learned that the most effective teachers over the centuries have used symbols, pictures, and stories to help make the most complex ideas a little less complicated, so I've included some of those as well.

Thanks for walking along with me as I offer some field-tested guidance. I hope you gain an idea or two that will help you roll up your sleeves and get back to living and leading, a little sooner than later, when life throws you the next curveball.

Michael Alan Tate

PREFACE

A man named Cyrus is about to learn a lot about a little-known fact of life: Change is not the same as transition. Perhaps you met Cyrus in my earlier book, *The White Shirt*.

If you haven't met Cyrus yet or learned about The White Shirt Strategy, here are some details that will help you as you follow along on this part of his journey.

At the beginning of the previous story, Cyrus and his three friends were participating in a kingdom ritual where they were given white shirts as part of their career designation, which represented a career chosen for them by someone else. This career wasn't a good fit for any of them.

Throughout the story, Cyrus develops a seven-step process for people to find the right fit, largely thanks to the wisdom and guidance of his dear mentor Darrius. Cyrus also takes some missteps along the way, particularly when he follows the advice of a fast-talking, shortcut-taker named Shadan.

As he completes the strategy Darrius and his wife Bina help him develop, Cyrus sets his focus on a symbol, the white shirt, because he believes that there's something about the white shirt itself that remains important.

As Cyrus said, "It's a white shirt because we're all called to do special work and use our talents in our unique way to make the world a better place. No talents are better than others. We have all been endowed with gifts by our Creator to use in this world. You can serve God no matter what you're doing. But it is more fulfilling and more beneficial for others if you are engaged in the work that satisfies your interests and uses your best talents that were born in you."

Those inborn talents and interests are represented by the color of the button selected for that white shirt. The following list shows you how various traits align:

The White Shirt Strategy Button System

Blue Buttons / A Thinker:
- gets results by planning and innovation
- likes to strategize, design, facilitate, and plan
- brings more beauty into the world

Red Buttons / A Doer:
- gets results by directing people to produce
- likes to build, oversee, and complete projects and get immediate, concrete results
- brings more action and products into the world

Yellow Buttons / A Protector:
- gets results by setting up systems and standards
- likes to develop standards/guidelines, control quality, analyze, and schedule
- brings more order into the world

Green Buttons / A Talker:
- gets results by involving and inspiring people
- likes to persuade, promote, sell, teach, coach, and negotiate
- brings more joy into the world

For Cyrus, the colored buttons became a simple way to identify and acknowledge the type of work people are designed to do, and the places we are most productive. For example, authors or artists would have blue buttons, carpenters – red buttons, accountants – yellow buttons, and salesmen – green buttons.

The plan considered the influence of parents, peers, and our pasts as we pursue meaningful work, and also helped individuals identify their invisible skills. Notably, this strategy was not used to pursue a specific job title but as a way to begin conversations and seek advice. One of the principles Cyrus learned and shared was: "Ask for a job, and you'll get advice. Ask for advice, and you'll get a job."

The good king that Cyrus served assigned him to formally develop this process and share it with the kingdom. As the kingdom citizens discovered the button color that was right for each of them and developed a one-page career plan based on the White Shirt strategy, they were able to find meaningful and fulfilling work.

And then what?

Cyrus and his friends are about to begin another journey, and I welcome you to follow along. By this time, they have used what they learned and helped many people find careers that are connected to the purpose that has been tugging at them from their earliest days. They will soon be reminded that finding a career path is not the end of the learning process, but will require an ability to adapt to changes around them as well as their roles within those changes.

This story begins about ten years after *The White Shirt* book concludes. Cyrus is married, has two children, and hears some news that causes him to stop, listen, and reassess life.

I welcome you to join Cyrus, Aaron, Bahram, and Gage as they learn the next important lessons in leadership and life: how to navigate when your world abruptly shifts on its axis.

CHAPTER ONE

The king convened the four leaders that he most trusted and sat with them at his royal table. Each man held a valuable role of service to his people. For it was through the White Shirt Strategy that individuals across the land could identify the gifts and talents that would lead to meaningful career paths as well as the process for connecting with a fulfilling work role.

The king glanced at the buttons on the white shirts worn by these trusted advisors, and he marveled again at what these colors had come to represent.

There was Aaron, whose career purpose was symbolized by the ruby red button (a Builder), which was a perfect fit for his role in overseeing palace engineering and construction. Bahram wore the emerald green button (for Talker), and he was thriving as the king's official spokesman and chancellor.

Gage's was the yellow gold button (a Planner), and he did a wonderful job keeping watch over the royal treasury. And Cyrus wore the blue button (for Thinker) and could never have found a more perfect calling than overseer of the White Shirt Strategy, a brilliant response to his own career struggles.

The king was most pleased in how well these men had served him over the last ten years, and he listened intently to the progress in their roles. All that he heard encouraged him, yet he also felt concerned. How should he prepare for what is ahead, whatever that may be?

He had always loved leading his people, yet he noticed that something within him was changing. It was harder to rise in the mornings. He was slower as he approached his throne. His memory was not as sharp. Ultimately, he was feeling older and a little less able to think as well as he had in his younger days.

As the discussion died down, the king looked reflectively toward the ceiling of his great palace. "It seems that life is always changing, doesn't it?" he said. "Take this palace, for instance. It's almost as if it has never been completed since construction began years and years ago. Oh, we certainly have the walls, floors, ceilings, and structure in place. But as soon as we finished building it, we began to start over on areas that had been worn down over the years." He laughed and said, "Kind of like me."

Those last words tickled his throat unexpectedly, which turned into a small cough, and that small cough turned into a coughing spell.

Cyrus quickly poured a glass of water from the pitcher on the table and offered it to the king. As the cough subsided, the king took a sip and regained his composure. "This cough has been with me for a few weeks now," he said with frustration. "It's nothing to worry about, but it's certainly annoying."

The leaders looked to each other as they held onto an unspoken question, "Was there truly nothing to worry about?"

"Now, where were we?" the king asked.

"We were talking about change, Sire," Gage answered helpfully. "And it's true what you said about this palace. The kingdom budget provides funds every year to make improvements and take care of the issues that arise, or else these structures would decay."

Aaron, glad the conversation was resuming after the coughing spell, added, "It has been so exciting to add the new improvements. Every year, we look for what we need to do next in our facilities, and we get ready for those changes."

Bahram had listened with uncharacteristic quietness until he found the right moment to add his enthusiastic view. "Change is a wonderful opportunity to get ready for new and exciting things," he said.

Then Cyrus brought the discussion home. "It's so rewarding to see all of this growth. In this building and in this kingdom, I love what is being created in people's lives."

Satisfied as he was, the king paused for a moment then gave voice to the questions that nagged him. "Gentlemen, let me ask you … how well would your areas perform if you weren't there every day? How would your workers handle that change?" He cleared his throat as he tried to hide a series of coughs that he quickly suppressed.

The men looked to each other as concern rose in their faces. Was the king planning to make a change that affected their jobs?

"I am so pleased with all you have done for me," the king continued. "Yet I just sense that it's time to roll up our sleeves and get to work preparing for our next phase. I have heard that some other kingdoms are making new changes and trying new things. I've received word that good things that have been happening under the leadership of a new queen, whose father passed away recently. Perhaps you four could take a trip and see what we can learn from her, or maybe not. That would be up to you. But I would like for each of you to think about how we could approach our next phase. I'm not asking for an answer now, but for you to think about this for the good of the kingdom."

The men nodded but felt unsettled by the direction these instructions could take.

The king continued, "Well, I have one more visitor to see before I return to my queen for the evening. I'm talking with a man who's been working on these issues with other kingdoms. In the meantime, take these thoughts with you as you return to your homes, and we will discuss them again soon."

"Yes, Sire," they said in unison.

Whenever they met with the king, they were reminded of the trust they had in this good leader, yet a concern about changes in the air was starting to rise. Given the king's age, they also did not feel they could dismiss the cough so easily.

Cyrus gathered the courage to ask out loud. "Do you think the king is in poor health?"

"Well, he does have a cough," Aaron said, "but I'm sure he's fine. There's been a lot of that going around."

"He probably needs to get a check-up with the kingdom physician," Gage added. "But let's not jump to conclusions."

"Yes," Bahram said, "he needs to take care of himself. He may need to relax more. But let's hope for the best."

With a sense of optimism slightly restored, the men said goodbye. Each took a different path home.

CHAPTER TWO

"The king's questions were interesting, but everything's going to be fine," Cyrus told himself as he walked across the palace grounds at a confident pace. He had been pursuing a purposeful career for years now, and he was certain that he would be able to navigate and assist in any issues the king wanted to address.

In fact, the afternoon meeting had stirred a dozen thoughts of the many individuals who had been helped with the White Shirt Strategy he and his friends had implemented. He recalled that moment late yesterday afternoon when Jahid stopped by the office to report on the first two weeks in a new job.

"I love what I'm doing," Jahid said. "It's almost as if the job I have was designed just for me, and in some ways it was. As you know, I had taken my plan to one of the people on the leadership team of my new company. Following your guidance, I didn't ask for a job. Instead, I showed the gentleman my one-page plan and asked for advice. Some weeks later, out of the blue, he sent for me again. He said that they had held a meeting and were talking about a need they had, and he thought of the skills I could bring to the table. So, they created this job and put me in it. Isn't that wonderful?"

"Yes, it truly is! I am so excited to hear of your great opportunity and how well it fits what you do best," Cyrus responded. He was never nonchalant when he heard how the White Shirt Strategy was making a difference in people's lives.

He'd seen another example just this morning when Parviz stopped him as they passed through the center of the kingdom. "I feel so fulfilled," Parviz said. "I had no idea how much the work I used to do was so draining and discouraging. I'm a lucky man to have been able to make this change at the middle point in my career."

He saw Teodoro as well, who said, "I finally feel that my contributions are genuinely of value. My superiors are recognizing my efforts more and more. But, frankly, even if no one noticed the good work I was doing, this idea of connecting to my purpose has been rewarding to me all on its own."

Cyrus continued his walk toward home as he said to himself, "I must never forget that I have the king to thank for these opportunities to be of service. If he hadn't recognized the value of what this could mean to his kingdom and to the people, I'd probably be sitting in a cave somewhere drawing on the walls."

He smiled to himself as he thought of the other great man who had helped him in that cave. His timely encounter with dear Darrius is where this personal career strategy had gotten its start. Darrius and his remarkable wife, Bina, were the ones who stepped in to give him guidance during that time when his greatest need was wisdom.

Cyrus had reached the street where his house was located when his neighbor Rafiq called out to him. "Cyrus! I have great news!"

"Tell me, Rafiq," Cyrus responded with a smile, "I love hearing great news."

Rafiq rushed to the gate that led to Cyrus's home. "I'm getting a promotion at work," Rafiq said. "I'm going to be in charge of a new department."

Cyrus slapped his neighbor's back in excitement. "That's wonderful," he said. "I knew you could do it."

"I know, but …"

"But what?"

"Well …" Rafiq stopped, then looked down.

"What is it?" Cyrus asked with a mix of curiosity and concern.

Rafiq continued. "Well, to tell you the truth, I'm anxious. I don't know how to manage people. And we have a lot of new things coming up." He exhaled as he let out this secret worry.

"Oh, you'll do fine," Cyrus said instinctively.

"Thank you for saying so," Rafiq said, shrugging and appearing uncertain.

"Don't worry," Cyrus emphasized, adding, "I am proud of you, my friend." As he headed toward his door, Cyrus had a moment where he wondered if he had been too quick to dismiss his neighbor's concern, but he brushed the thought aside. In fact, this conversation and even the one with the king were quickly forgotten a short time later when Cyrus faced more urgent news.

Walking inside, he found his wife, Hester, holding a letter. After they greeted each other with a warm kiss, she said, "I arrived at home just ahead of you and look, this has come for you." As she extended the envelope toward Cyrus, he recognized Bina's handwriting at once. Opening the letter, he began to read unhappy news about his dear friend Darrius.

"He's ill," Cyrus said to Hester. "I must go to him."

"I'm so sorry. Yes, of course. You must go. Don't worry about a thing here. The children and I will manage. You know we will miss you, but this is important."

Cyrus thought for another moment. "I'd like to ask Aaron, Bahram, and Gage to join me."

"Actually," Hester said, "I would feel better myself if they went along with you. I don't want you to make this journey alone, and they are the best ones to share it with you."

That evening, Cyrus went off to find his lifelong friends and to share the heartrending news. The others and their wives were quick to agree to this journey. The next day, Aaron, Bahram, and Gage met Cyrus at the palace and requested to speak to the king about their impending absence.

Soon, their audience was granted, and they revealed the news of their friend's illness. "Darrius …" the king said his name thoughtfully. "I am appreciative of the impact he has had on this kingdom and its people."

The king smiled toward his four loyal subjects. "Go to Darrius," he said. "Go, with my blessing."

"Thank you, Sire," Cyrus said as they all bowed before their king.

As they walked out, Cyrus thought he noticed a familiar face in the king's waiting area. "Could that be … Shadan?" he asked himself. "No, surely not," he answered, quickly dismissing the idea.

He recalled his earlier encounters with this schemer and keenly remembered Shadan's focus on easy paths to good fortune. Cyrus was confident the king would never agree to meet with a man of such unsavory character. Yet he had to check this out.

He walked back toward the king's waiting area. "Shadan?" he called out to test his theory. A well-dressed head turned toward his voice.

"Yes?" the gentleman asked.

"It is you," Cyrus said. "You're Shadan, the one I met years ago when I was looking for help finding a career."

"Perhaps we have met, but I do not recall," Shadan said solemnly as he shrugged.

"You don't remember me?" Cyrus asked.

"Oh, I'm sorry, friend. I meet so many people in my line of work. I'm afraid it's hard to keep everyone straight. These days a lot of people are using my name to get in to see kings … so …" Shadan shrugged again.

Cyrus was incensed by the implied insult. "I don't need to use your name to see our king. But I do remember you, and I can tell, you haven't changed a bit." He almost spit out the words, "You take care, Shadan." And good riddance, he thought to himself.

"Thank you, and it's actually Sir Shadan now. I have been knighted in several kingdoms since we last met."

"Oh, so you do remember me?" Cyrus realized Shadan had just revealed himself.

"Well, perhaps I do. You seem familiar. I hope you are doing well these days."

"I am indeed," Cyrus said. Then he turned and walked away, ending this conversation with the curtness it deserved.

CHAPTER THREE

The next morning, Aaron, Bahram, Gage, and Cyrus packed their provisions and clothing, loaded bundles on their donkeys, and said goodbye to their families. Each one was thinking about the good times they shared in their past and even some of the not-so-good times. It is interesting how an exit from the comfort of the day to day, can rock the emotions of brave men.

As Cyrus prepared for his departure, his mind wandered to his and Hester's wedding and the birth of each of their children. Then he snapped back to reality and kissed his family goodbye, as the others did the same.

The friends hoisted themselves atop the donkeys for the long ride. It had been years since they had spent so much time together, just the four of them. Their conversations were a rambling mix of stories about their families, anecdotes from their workplaces, and memories of their boyhoods.

As the sun began to ease below the nearby mountain, they unloaded and set up camp by a river for the night. Then they gathered around the fire that Aaron had built.

"I expect that it will take us over a week to reach Jerusalem and then only half a day to reach Darrius's home in Bethlehem," Gage said. "So, we should start again at first light and keep our pace."

"That's fine," Aaron said. "We don't want to waste time getting there."

The men shared a quick meal of grapes, cheese, and bread. As they ate, Bahram said, "This reminds me of when we were kids. We were always outdoors, under the stars and near the river. We always talked of crossing the river."

"*You* did, Bahram," Aaron interjected. "When we'd done as much as we'd thought to do, you would come up with one more thing for us to do."

"Yes, when it was time to head for home," Gage remembered, "you would always come up with something else, like crossing the river."

Bahram shrugged, "I wanted to cross the river."

Gage held up his hands. "But we had no boat, the current was too strong, and if we had tried to wade or swim, we don't know where we would have ended up."

"If we were to go back to that same river, I bet I could cross it now," Bahram said with a smile.

"Ah, but it won't be the same river," Cyrus added.

"What are you talking about?" Aaron asked somewhat impatiently. "The river is still there."

Cyrus explained, "What I mean is, there's a saying that you can never enter the same river twice. Everything is always changing. The water doesn't stay in the same place; thus, it is not the same river. Things are flowing in and flowing out."

Gage added, "Don't forget that changes in the river, like with a storm, can produce big waves to battle."

Bahram said, "Very well. Your point is taken. We will cross a different river," He continued with a smile, "But I am confident that we can use what we've learned to figure out how to cross a river that we couldn't cross when we were younger, even if there are big scary waves to contend with, Gage."

"Indeed," Aaron echoed, "We can do whatever we set our minds to do."

Gage banked the fire as he called the discussion to a close. "The morning will be here soon, my friends. Tomorrow, we have a lot of ground to cover. Let us get the rest we need. The river can wait."

The four leaned back on their bedding and prepared for rest. Cyrus spoke one last thought as he gazed upward. "The stars are so beautiful tonight," he mused. "It reminds me of how much can happen that we don't even realize. Somehow things work together, as if by an intricate design, for us to achieve our purpose. Good night, my friends."

CHAPTER FOUR

After a few days of riding and catching up on life events, family happenings, and political opinions, quietness enveloped the men as they drew closer to their destination. Each was contemplating what they would soon face, and they were reluctant to speak their thoughts, as men so often are.

Not surprisingly, Bahram, the talker of the bunch, broke the silence. "Guys, I'm not sure how I'll handle it if Darrius dies," he said. In this in-your-face manner, Bahram broke the code of imagined despair for the group.

Aaron, Gage, and Cyrus responded in unison: "Me either." It was as if the door that was being held tightly closed had suddenly flown open.

Cyrus added, "We have all experienced loss … some of us a parent, a close relative, or friend. What if we think about what that was like and what we learned about ourselves, then that might help us serve Bina and others when we arrive."

Bahram agreed. "Yes, I know we're assuming and expecting the worst to happen, even if we're hoping against hope that it doesn't."

Aaron began to speak, slowly but deliberately. "I have a hard time thinking about things like this. I really don't know how I felt or what I did when my favorite uncle passed away last year. It was a blur and maybe it still is."

Gage, the keen observer, asked, "Would you like to hear what I saw, Aaron?"

"Of course," his friend replied.

"You did something surprising, almost the opposite of what would have been expected knowing your personality."

"Go on."

"You got started on a crazy project. You got busy tearing up a perfectly good wall in your back yard and building a new one. You were not focused on anything productive. Then one day a few weeks later, you showed up as the old Aaron, out front, telling all of us what to do."

Bahram and Cyrus nodded their concurrence.

Aaron offered a knowing smile. "Yeah, I remember. I just felt like I should stay busy. No matter how weird my efforts appeared, the project helped me to get my mind off my loss and me. Soon I was helping others get things done. In all that, I guess I let go of the past, and I found myself again."

Cyrus asked, "What about you, Gage? What has been a loss for you?"

Gage responded, "Oh, I had a difficult, painful loss for sure. You probably remember, I had a cousin contract a terrible disease and pass away several years back, and I'm still not over it. We were the same age and really close. It was tough. Did you notice anything about my reaction?"

Bahram spoke up. "I sure did. You were so angry."

"Really? Did it show?" Gage asked.

"I'll say," Bahram acknowledged. "I thought you might get yourself in trouble or hurt someone. Your actions showed little concern for the people around you."

"Ouch," Gage said.

"You mistreated your donkey, riding him at breakneck speed. The poor beast eventually collapsed. You were short tempered, barking at people over the least little thing. It's better now, but to tell you the truth, it's hard to get that picture of you out of my mind. I saw you yelling at your kids, and I was very concerned about you, and about them. One time, I even saw you yell at your family dog. I seriously thought you were going to kick him."

Gage breathed out a painful sigh. "Yeah, it was a hard time. I am so sorry for my actions. I knew what I was doing but could not control myself."

Bahram continued, "But you seem so much like your old self now, so detailed, so ready to analyze everything. What did you do to get yourself back?"

Gage said, "I didn't know what to do until Cyrus mentioned I might consider writing down how I really felt about losing my cousin. He was deeply involved because this is also his family now that I'm married to his sister Taavi, and he's my brother-in-law."

Cyrus added, "Yeah, and your wife pleaded with me to help you, both as my family and as my friend, and I was going to do what I could."

Gage continued, "Well, you did help because the suggestion worked. Writing helps me let go of my negative thoughts and talk about those things with Taavi. She listens uncondition-ally to me and doesn't try to fix me. It was shocking how her kind ear drew us closer than we have ever been. And like her mother before her, she prays often. In fact, she posted a saying on our kitchen wall: *When life gives you more than you can stand — kneel!* I wonder if kneeling more often *before* life knocks me down might be a better approach?"

Gage's voice trailed off into a thoughtful silence. The men let the silence continue for only a few more moments. Then Bahram said, "OK, guys, I know this is touchy stuff and it's hard for us as men, but we've got to get through this before we get to the house. So, talk."

Cyrus smiled. "Bahram, you started this thing. Why have you, our unrelenting storyteller, been so quiet?"

Bahram shrugged. "Well, even as outgoing as I seem with my feelings on my sleeve to most everybody else, I really need order in the background to be who I am. Give me time, lots of time alone, to be my loud self. But I'll tell you about this terrible experience. My biggest loss and grieving time happened when I made some bad financial decisions. I almost lost my home a few years back. My wife, Deborah, was so frustrated she told me to leave. I didn't see my family for months."

"What?" Aaron said. "I had no idea."

"I didn't know either," Gage added.

"News to me too," Cyrus said, shaking his head.

Bahram continued, "Of course I hid it all and kept my image up. But inside I was torn apart and had terrible headaches and stomach problems. I may have looked fine on the outside, but I was torn up inside. I kept asking, "Why, why me, why now?" I even considered suicide. Then I ran into a few men who had experienced much of the same trouble I had, in one way or another. They listened and helped me process my pride and spoke the truth, but only when I asked them."

"But things are OK now?" Cyrus asked.

"Yes, I'm back with my family and am now more open with Deborah. We are closer and believe it or not, as Gage said, I'm learning to kneel more."

"Who would have thought it?" Gage asked with a kind grin.

Cyrus was baffled. How had they not known about each other's tough times? Bahram interrupted his deep thought. "OK, spit it out, Cy. Your turn."

Cyrus sat up straight and spoke with care. "All of you know about Hester's miscarriage two years and three months ago. Like Bahram said, I couldn't stop asking myself *why? Why us?* I never talked about it with any of you. I'd say that was because I didn't want to burden you. So, I started asking myself, 'Who is to blame for this?' I got angry with the midwife. I blamed her and God. I would not let it out because I thought it would make me look weak. My pride kept me from being honest, so I poured myself into my work, avoiding everyone, even Hester, until Darrius asked me, 'When are you going to grieve over your lost child?' His words hit hard, and I was furious. I yelled at him in response, but then I fell apart. He loved me enough to risk our relationship to try to help me. He cared enough to listen and was smart enough to offer no advice. I broke down in his arms, and it all poured out."

Cyrus continued, "Thinking back to that time of loss and how I felt and acted so frozen and terrified," he paused in thought, adding, "I just realized how much my grief felt like fear. It was akin to my reaction to the sight of waves crashing unpredictably on a stormy river, as Gage mentioned before."

Cyrus pulled out his journal and drew

WAVES OF FEAR

They studied the picture in a moment of silence, until Aaron spoke again.

CHAPTER FIVE

"Do you remember what we learned in our first journey about how you can't feel your way into acting, but if you take an action, good feelings will follow?" Aaron asked. The others answered affirmatively, and Aaron continued. "I wonder if that applies to feelings of fear and grief?"

Cyrus shrugged as he replied, "Aaron, that is way beyond what I know, but it is something we should be considering."

Gage said, "It seems like there must be something we could learn from this conversation that could help others like us handle changes in life in a better way."

Aaron added, "Well, what I have learned is that in the midst of big change or loss, the worst counselor you can listen to is yourself."

"What does that mean?" Gage asked.

"You know how it is," Aaron began, "we tend to think we're so smart we can figure stuff out on our own, but when times are really tough, we don't have enough distance from the situation to provide our own wisdom. So, basically, in a bad time, you are your worst counselor. Remember, this is key to the White Shirt Strategy, to find a friend to work with when you need to change careers. The principle of 'two are better that one' may be true for most of the changes we experience in life."

They all nodded and rode on in silence, each considering what all this might mean.

The afternoon sun was hot, and the ride was taking longer than they expected. When they saw the stream, they were glad. They stopped so that they and the animals could take a break and get a drink of water.

As the others talked near the animals, Cyrus walked a short distance away and pulled out his journal. Usually this was his end-of-the-day routine, but he knew that tonight he would be too tired to think. He wrote in the journal "When people experience unexpected life interruptions, they can easily get stuck in *Why* and *Who*." Then he penned Aaron's words, "When you are stressed, you are your worst counselor."

After a brief break, they mounted up again and rode at a faster pace toward Jerusalem.

An hour after dark, they arrived at an inn where Cyrus had worked many years ago, before he'd made his move to Bethlehem. Several people who had worked with him were still there. Delighted old friends greeted Cyrus and his friends. They all felt right at home.

The architecture of the inn had changed a lot since Cyrus had been there. They had even added a second floor. But the spirit of hospitality was as inviting as ever. After a tour of the updated lodge and meeting with the rest of the staff, the new manager suggested a nearby place for dinner, and the four walked to a small café. Over dinner they talked about the life-giving atmosphere they had just experienced, because it was so uncommon in most lodging houses in those days. They wondered how the manager maintained that healthy culture and positive feeling in the staff.

After they'd completed their meal, they returned to say goodnight and to talk to the manager about the environment. He was not out front. Cyrus peeked in his office and saw it was empty as well. Then he noticed the room next to the manager's office was open. It looked like a break room with tables set up for the staff to meet or eat a meal. Stepping in, he noticed two pieces of parchment on the wall. One was a neatly printed list of ten things. A few inches below the list was a handwritten quote, which was penned in large letters. He called to his friends, "Hey, you need to see this."

The others joined him in the room and took note of the large poster-like documents. Of the four, Gage seemed most mesmerized by the detailed list of staff expectations:

◆ ◆ ◆

1. Love your job with all your heart—or find another job you can love.
2. Walk in your customer's sandals, before making a decision about them.
3. Leave every room spotless and leave everything in its place.
4. Wash your hands when you leave one guest room and enter another.

5. Never blame a guest or another team member for a problem.
6. Try not to make the same mistake twice—fix it well the first time.
7. Never talk to or eat with your friends in a guest's presence.
8. Do not steal items from the inn or take pay for work you did not do.
9. Gossip is not allowed at work. (See rule #1, part 2.)
10. End each guest interaction on a high note!

Everyone has unseen battles they are fighting. Be kind!

♦ ♦ ♦

For his part, Aaron was transfixed by the handwritten words in bold print at the bottom of the parchment poster. He read them aloud. "Everyone has unseen battles they are fighting. Be kind!"

As the men were talking about the messages on the wall, the manager walked in. Grinning, he slapped Cyrus on the back and asked, "Well what do you fellows think about my ten workplace expectations list? Or, as the staff likes to call it, my ten rules of perfect perfection."

They all laughed. "Funny you should ask," Cyrus responded. "We came looking for you to inquire as to how you keep your staff enthused and keep your service so excellent. I hope you don't mind that we peeked in here."

"I'm glad you did," said the manager. "As you can imagine, it was not easy on my people when I began."

"I put the list of expectations up first, and that was all I had in here. Some of the staff got upset because they said the work expectations were too harsh. I got to thinking about that and realized they had a point. Then I found the other saying which has helped me as their manager to stop and think before I judge an employee's behavior when he or she misses the mark."

He paused to gather his thoughts, and then continued, "Sometimes people act out in an unproductive way because something has happened in their life. They're not bad people; they're just carrying a heavy load from another relationship or stressful place in their life. I found that if I suspend judgment and ask what's going on and listen, most people come back around to being and doing their best."

Gage interjected, "But clear expectations are necessary. Good workers like to know what is expected otherwise there is chaos, and everybody suffers."

The manager said, "I couldn't agree with you more. You try to maintain this balancing act between accountability and caring. When it's done right, people will have the commitment and enthusiasm to roll up their sleeves, get to work, and work together."

"True words," Bahram said.

"True indeed," Aaron agreed.

"This is leadership wisdom we all could use," Bahram said as the men turned toward the stairs.

During their walk to their rooms, each man, in his own way, was reliving their travel conversations, contemplating the message they just talked about, and considering what they might face tomorrow.

It was a fitful night of tossing and turning.

CHAPTER SIX

T he next morning, they rose at sunrise but not to the brightness they expected. Gray clouds drifted across the sky, though the sun peeked in and out when given the chance. Cyrus hoped this was not a sign of how the day might play out. However, he put those thoughts aside, dressed in his white shirt, and carefully fastened his blue buttons. The others were waiting as he walked in the lobby, and they too wore white shirts, though with green, gold, or red buttons. They were ready to see Darrius.

The last leg of the trip didn't take long. It was mid-afternoon when they arrived at Darrius's door. Fearing the possibility they could be too late, Cyrus took a moment to steady his nerves. Then he lifted the heavy doorknocker and released it. The door opened and Bina's bright smile illuminated the doorway. Her warm hugs for all of them let Cyrus know they had not missed their chance.

"Darrius rallied at the very thought of your visit," Bina explained as she escorted the younger men inside. "It is as if he willed himself to a moment of strength just to see your face again. He is napping now but should awaken soon."

Cyrus was deeply moved, for he knew how much Darrius meant to him, but to think that he meant as much to Darrius was indeed humbling.

As the men approached the bedroom door, Aaron said to Cyrus, "You go in first. We'll wait out here until you speak to him." Cyrus nodded with appreciation for the respect Aaron was showing for his relationship with Darrius. The others held back while Cyrus entered the room and saw his dear friend in a restful slumber.

As Cyrus drew near, Darrius stirred, opening his eyes. He blinked a couple of times as if to get a clearer view of the face in front of him. Then he managed a slight smile as he spoke in a far weaker voice than Cyrus remembered. "For a moment, I thought I was seeing a vision, but you appear to be real."

"Oh, I am real," Cyrus, answered.

"It is wonderful to see you again, though I apologize for not getting out of bed to greet you more properly."

"I just had to come to see you when I heard you weren't well. Nothing could have kept me away."

"Thank you, my son. Tell me, how are you? How are Hester and the children?"

"Just wonderful. Everybody's doing very well." He paused and added with a smile, "Little Darrius, especially, is a treasure."

Darrius returned the smile. "That is one of my greatest honors, knowing that one of your children carries my name."

"All of us who know you carry more than that," Cyrus said. "We carry your influence and your teachings, and we have shared these things with many others."

"I learned a lot in my long life," Darrius said philosophically. "I am glad it is not going to waste."

"Though your body may be weaker than you'd like, your influence is still very strong. That's why we have traveled as fast as possible to get here. When we heard that you were ill, we knew we had to come."

"We?" Darrius asked. "Who is with you?"

"Aaron, Bahram, and Gage joined me on this journey. They wanted to see you, too."

"Oh, how marvelous. You're all here," Darrius said. "Please bring them in. I would love to see them."

Cyrus stood, walked toward the doorway, and motioned for the others to enter. They soon gathered in front of the elderly man's bed as Darrius took in this sight. "My sons, if not by blood, certainly by the heart we have shared over many years." Suddenly he noticed their garments. "Look at those beautiful shirts," he said. Tears of pride filled his eyes.

Aaron cleared his throat. "Darrius, I think of you often and always with gratitude. With your help, I built a career, a family, and a treasure to take care of them."

Bahram interjected, "I think of you with joy. My work is so much fun, and I get to share it with others."

Gage added his own thoughts. "I am grateful to you for helping put the pieces into place for the life I now lead. I couldn't have done it without you. None of us could have."

Darrius's face relaxed, exuding warmth. "You all are so kind, and I rejoice at how well you are doing." He paused then added, "We took quite a journey, didn't we? I wish I could see more of it with you. I can't help but be reminded of Moses."

"Moses?" Cyrus asked, curiously.

"Moses is a man who is very important to my faith tradition. He led his people—my people—through a wilderness over a long period of time, but he did not live long enough to arrive with them at their final destination. Even so, all who follow my faith tradition carry with them the teachings God gave Moses to this day." Darrius paused for a moment to gain strength to continue his thoughts, then spoke again. "Similarly, I won't get to see all that you do, but I hope you will remember me and the lessons we learned together."

"Indeed, we will," Cyrus responded solemnly. "Indeed, we will."

Gage interrupted, "Darrius, we should let you save your strength. You should rest. We'll be here in the morning, and we will talk again then."

"We'll have so many wonderful stories to tell you," Bahram added.

"Good night, dear Darrius," Aaron said. "We will see you in the morning."

Darrius closed his eyes and smiled as they tiptoed out of the room.

CHAPTER SEVEN

B ina showed the men to their guest rooms in the beautiful home she shared with her life mate. "I've prepared dinner," she said as she turned to go, "so please join me in the dining room when you've had a chance to freshen up."

Soon, the four friends were at her table, enjoying her wonderful hospitality as they shared stories of their families and their lives.

"It means so much to me that you have journeyed all this way to say goodbye."

"Goodbye? Are you sure?" Bahram said in protest. "He looks weak, but couldn't he recover?"

"Yes, but this is a good day. Tomorrow may not be a good day. We never know."

"Is there anything we can do?" Aaron asked. "We know many physicians in our kingdom, and they have the latest training."

"There may be a regimen of care that will restore him to health," Gage added.

Bina shook her head. "I am a hopeful person by nature, but I know better than to ignore the fact that losses come into every life and eventually every situation. Mourning is part of our time here. Yet, in that grief, there is hope."

The men nodded and kept their thoughts to themselves as the reality of what was ahead registered more deeply.

"Well, my friends, I am tired," Bina, said. "I will check on my dear love once more, then turn in for the evening." The men stood as she prepared to leave the table. She nodded to them as she added, "I am sure you are all exhausted from your travels. Rest well, and I will see you in the morning."

A short time later, Cyrus was in the room that had been prepared for him. He took out a journal and made a few notes about his day, including what he was most grateful for and what he was least grateful for. This nightly habit had stayed with him since his mother's reminder during that long journey when he first encountered Darrius. The first entry was easy. "I am most grateful for the visit I had with my cherished friend. I am so fortunate that I have had the opportunity to see him again."

The second took more reflection: "I am least grateful for how he has changed since I last saw him. He's so weak, he didn't get out of bed. Where is that energy that ran circles around me even when I was a third his age? I wish he could be as he always was."

Cyrus closed his notebook, suspecting that his last wish was something that was never meant to be. He settled in for a deep, restful sleep. The next morning, he woke early, taking a moment to remember where he was as he opened his eyes in an unfamiliar place. Then he rose quickly and dressed for the day.

"Good morning, Cyrus," Bina said as she met him in the kitchen. "Please help yourself to coffee, sweet bread, and fruit and tell the others. I'll be in with Darrius. Come in whenever you're ready."

Moments later, Aaron, Bahram, and Gage joined Cyrus at the kitchen table. After a quick breakfast, Aaron asked Cyrus, "Will you see how he's doing? That's why we're here, after all."

"Yes," Cyrus agreed. He hadn't wanted to rush or disturb Bina's time with Darrius, but Aaron was right. These moments were precious, and they needed to make the most of them. He knocked lightly on the door.

Bina answered, "Please come in."

As the four entered the room, Darrius seemed so weak, so fragile, as if he were already too far away. But a moment later, he stirred, and his eyes opened. He steadied his gaze on these men, and he rose up on his arms. They tried to stop him, but he held up his hand and waved them off.

"Sit down," he said. His voice was suddenly strong and his mind clear. He was their teacher again and his one last lesson poured forth. "Sometime during the night, it all became clear to me what I needed to say to you."

"We are grateful for anything you would tell us," Cyrus said. "But please do not tax yourself."

"Let me continue," Darrius said, dismissing the concern. "There is something you need to know for your future work and to help my family over the next few days. I mentioned Moses yesterday, but the story of Moses and the exodus of our people is more than a story about my faith and history. It also teaches us about the difference between change and transition. Change is the loss event, the act that has happened. Transition is the feelings or emotions people go through when they experience change.

"As young leaders you will need to understand this concept so you can guide people to move through transition in a healthy way. When people are in the emotions of transition, they are not themselves. They can act in irrational ways or may appear 'out of their right mind.' This is natural. They are going through the first phases of transition. Each person walks, or more appropriately, wanders along their emotional transition path in their own way. There are several other phases you will need to learn about. Your job as a leader is to learn about transition and how to guide people to make it through their wilderness of emotions to their promised land, as we say in our faith."

Darrius coughed deep and fell back to his bed. "Pay close attention to people when change happens. Watch and learn. You will need to know this sooner than you think." He looked at them as one making his last desperate throw of dice at life, and he whispered, "Great leaders are great listeners."

Darrius closed his eyes. The others didn't speak, but they shared a knowing look. Each realized time was short, yet they were not yet prepared for what they would be called upon to do. How would they help others through transition if they didn't even know how to do it themselves? As Darrius had said, they would need to learn fast, for they could also see that the one who could best teach them would soon depart.

Darrius's eyes remained closed as his breathing became more labored. "His rally seems to have ended," Bina acknowledged. "This may not be one of his good days. I will send for our children."

Cyrus had a lump in his throat as he asked, "What do we do?"

"Talk to him. He will hear you, and it will be medicine for his soul."

The men pulled their chairs closer and one by one began telling stories of their memories of their first meetings with Darrius, of the times they had shared together, and of the lessons they had learned that they would never forget. They could see a flicker of his eyelids, or a small smile on his face, or feel a squeeze of his hand, and they knew he was still with them.

When his son and daughter and grandchildren arrived, the men stepped out to give the family time together. Then they returned in the late hours, as the moments seemed to be drawing even nearer to Darrius's transition into the eternal world. Finally, that moment came.

And Darrius breathed his last.

CHAPTER EIGHT

T he custom for Darrius's faith tradition was that the funeral service would occur the day a person passed away, but since it was so late in the evening, it was planned for the following day. Someone would sit with the body until that time. Cyrus and his friends each took a turn sitting with Darrius to give the family a break as they made funeral preparations.

The service was held early the next day and led by the teacher from the temple and a few close friends. Cyrus was one of the speakers and, as the teacher had advised, kept his memories to a few words. Aaron, Bahram, Gage, and he all served as pall-bearers along with other family members. Then Darrius's simple wooden casket was buried in the family's cemetery plot, as an amazing life reached its end.

Yet his influence would continue for a long, long time.

The four friends stayed the rest of that day and the evening in honor of their friend, and in support of the family. They observed family members in mourning and noticed the different ways each one worked through their loss. Most were sad, in shock, or sat alone; a few were loud and often a little too outspoken. Some became counselors to others, listening to the mourners as they processed their emotions.

Later Cyrus realized that he and his friends had observed some of the same reactions at this funeral that they had talked about during their trip to be with Darrius.

Cyrus, always the thinker, began to notice that the mourners seemed to be helped more by those who asked questions and listened to them, than by those who gave advice. Most surprisingly was the teacher's approach. He seemed to know that many people were searching for an answer to why this good man was taken away. He listened intently then asked them if they had experienced a loss of a family member in their past. Most had. Then he inquired, "How did you get through that loss?" Cyrus could see the realization in their eyes when they sensed they had inner resources to get through this loss as well.

Before the teacher walked away from each person, he usually asked something like, "Why don't you think about what you can do to help someone who is struggling today?" Cyrus watched in amazement, as one grieving person after another was guided one small step at a time toward healing. Although some were too distraught to have this restorative conversation, most people left the teacher's presence in a more positive frame of mind.

Cyrus not only observed the teacher facilitate this spirit of healing, he also experienced it as the teacher guided him in his own grief. Applying this insight, Cyrus began to model his helpful approach with others that day by:

Listening to their back-story, that is, hearing their *Whys*;

Asking *How* they got through a similar change in their past; and…

Inquiring *What* they could do to help another person. He made an extra note, *"Helping another person get through their struggle can help you get through yours."*

Cyrus also noticed one other action the teacher had taken. After he completed the funeral service, the teacher made a point to wash his hands, dipping his hands into a basin of water and patting them dry with a clean cloth. This seemed to be an act that meant more than having clean hands, and during their conversation, Cyrus asked the teacher about this part of the ceremony.

"It is our custom to wash our hands after attending a funeral," the teacher explained. "There are many views associated with this custom, such as purifying ourselves for the life ahead or finding protection from negative forces that may try to fill a void when a loved one dies. But what I also think is important is to recognize an ending. We have honored a loss, and we have said goodbye. By washing our hands, we are saying that we will now move forward with a fresh, clean start."

Cyrus made one more note:

Help people acknowledge *When* there has been an ending, so they could decide to begin anew.

The crowd dwindled and farewells and well-wishes faded in the distance as people headed back home. The four men lingered over their goodbyes to Bina and promised to keep in touch. The family had packed them some food for their journey.

At midday, they finally loaded their donkeys with all their bundles, and hoisted themselves up for the long ride home. They traveled along, in silence, for a few hours. Before the full end of the day took them over, Cyrus asked that they stop for the night a little early. He wanted there to be enough daylight left for them to fulfill a request.

"We have been through an important, even a pivotal experience," he said to the others. "I know we all sense this, yet I think we would waste the opportunity we have if we don't acknowledge what we have learned. Before another evening falls, I would like for us to take the time to record our thoughts about what has taken place. What we are going through everyone goes through, and we may be able to help people learn about the steps they need to take next in situations like we've just experienced."

The men set up camp for the night and took the paper Cyrus provided to make their notes. No one could sleep, since their minds were too busy and their hearts were too tender. They wrote, but also took breaks to talk.

"I want to do this better this time," Gage said with sincerity. "When my cousin died, I did not handle it very well." His friends nodded, knowing his words were true. "All that anger was misdirected. I was just really hurting, and I needed to admit it so I could move on."

"Yeah," Aaron agreed, "my response to my uncle's loss was different than Gage's, but I still sense that it wasn't healthy. Instead of staying busy, I wish I'd acknowledged that I was sad for him, for the cousins who lost their dad, for my mother who lost her brother, and for me who lost someone I really admired."

Bahram said, "Sometimes it's okay to just be sad."

Cyrus summed up the idea they were expressing. "I'm thinking we'll all find something in how we managed our past times of change that can tell us, for better or for worse, how we might move forward now." His mind went back to the teacher's questions in the wake of the funeral.

The next morning, they were thoughtful and reflective as they prepared to continue their journey. They didn't get far when their thoughts were interrupted by the activity they saw as they arrived in Jerusalem.

Shops were closing as storekeepers, tradespeople, and salespeople appeared to be leaving for home. One man nodded as he greeted the four travelers. "Hello," he said.

"Hello," Bahram said in return. "The city seems to be closing. Is everything okay?"

"Ah, you must not be familiar with our traditions. This is a special holiday for our faith, and we are headed to our homes for the Meal of Remembrance."

"Meal of Remembrance?" Aaron repeated.

"The Meal of Remembrance is a special meal, a festive celebration that reminds us of what God has done for us and how his servant Moses led our people out of the foreign land to our promised land," the man explained. "Have you a place to share this special event?"

"No, we don't," Gage said. "We are traveling through town."

"Well, my name is Samuel," the man said. "My family would be pleased if you would join us for our Meal of Remembrance."

Cyrus looked quickly to the others before accepting Samuel's invitation. "We would be pleased to join you," he answered. "My name is Cyrus, and these are my friends, Bahram, Aaron, and Gage."

"It is my honor to welcome you to be a part of my family's celebration."

The men followed Samuel to his home, where they were welcomed again by many family members of every age. Samuel was a gracious host, as was his wife, and everyone made an extra effort to tend to their unexpected guests.

The meal itself was served in an orderly, ceremonial fashion, and as Cyrus took note, the steps were well known to the family members and carefully followed. The visitors also heard a fuller account of the story of the Passover, the Exodus, and Moses, the Divinely chosen leader for the people of Israel.

From what Cyrus learned, their ancestors were living in a foreign land in those days, but not by choice. After being in this land, they had prospered and been well fed during a time of famine. Some were business leaders, and some held positions of power. But the leadership of the foreign land and its culture had changed over time. Now they found themselves living as slaves to a dictator who was harsh and difficult.

Oddly, though their situation was unjust, the people had become accustomed to the system that was in place. They were afraid and made no attempt to leave their situation until God called Moses to be their leader. Even then, the system had a strong hold on the people, and they were uncertain about going forward. What's more, the harsh ruler refused every offer Moses made to him in an effort to negotiate the freedom of his people.

Because he refused to let them leave, the leader himself did not fare well. He began to suffer greatly from his stubborn resistance. He liked things just as they were, and he intended to keep it that way, at great cost to himself, his family, and everyone in that foreign land. Then God exacted a final dramatic event that broke the king's harsh spirit, and his people were told to leave.

This story, it seemed to Cyrus, was remarkable on its face. The God of the universe had reached down to rescue this group of people from a terrible injustice, and He used an ordinary man to take leadership over this great exodus. Cyrus couldn't help but sense that there would be some important applications he and his friends could adopt in the work they were being called to do, just as Darrius had said.

CHAPTER NINE

When the Meal of Remembrance was done, Cyrus said to Samuel, "Thank you for sharing your special meal and family time with us. We learned a lot."

Samuel responded, "We were honored to have you as our guests."

Cyrus continued, "Our friend Darrius had told us that there were principles in this story that would help us become better leaders. Could you tell us more about what happened after your people got out of the foreign land and were in the wilderness? I think your observations would help us understand more about transition that individuals and even groups of people go through."

Sensing the importance of this request, Samuel said, "It would be my pleasure." Samuel excused himself from his family and asked the men to follow him. They sat at an outside table, in a quiet place away from the crowd as the setting sun and rising moon provided enough light for their discussion. Cyrus, Aaron, Bahram, and Gage had their journals open and pens in hand.

Samuel began, "Our people were not just running away from their past. They were running towards their promised land, a place of peace and prosperity. But it was not a simple, easy journey. It actually took around forty years."

The four looked up in surprise as Samuel continued. "After our people had gotten a few days outside the walls of the foreign land, the angry ruler changed his mind and commanded his army to bring them back at once. In hot pursuit, his soldiers caught sight of them near a large body of water. As the soldiers advanced, our people were trapped with the king's soldiers behind them and the deep water in front. After intense prayer, Moses stretched his hand out over the water, and God miraculously opened up a path in the sea. With steady walls of water on the left and right, our people walked through the sea on dry land and made it to the other side as the soldiers pursued them. Safely on shore, our people looked back and saw the waters close in and drown the full army of the king. This event ended my people's past and moved them forward without fear of being taken back."

The men were enthralled. Cyrus began to sketch as Gage said, "It's interesting how water is often involved with endings and new beginnings." The others scribbled notes.

Samuel continued, "Yes, and this event with the sea was good news and bad news. It was good news in that they had a new start and they were free to be who they were called to be. It was bad news in that they were in the desert, and the food and water they had brought along quickly disappeared. There were few provisions in this harsh land. Yet, once again, God sent a series of miracles and provided both food and water. Things were good for a while, but soon the people's emotions took over again. They complained about having to eat the same old food. They got angry that the tents were not like their real houses. They even argued and bargained with Moses to take them back to the foreign land, remembering only the good times there."

Cyrus interrupted, "They wanted to return to their lives as slaves?"

"Yes," Samuel said, "They were confused because this transition was hard. Our leader realized they had forgotten who they were again. Confusion and chaos will always carry the day when people forget their purpose."

Cyrus added thoughtfully, "Well, I remember from personal experience how lost I felt when my purpose wasn't clear, and I did miss my old life even when I knew it wasn't the right fit. So, I guess it's like when you don't know where you are, you want to return to something familiar, even if it wasn't a good situation."

Samuel nodded. "The stories of our people are always teaching us. When they were confused and unsure, Moses reminded them that they were chosen with a purpose, and they would get through this wilderness and get to the 'land of milk and honey' if they trusted God."

"Milk and honey?" Bahram said, "I like the sound of that."

"Yes, it's a word picture of what it will feel like when we pursue and find our purpose, the Promised Land. However, Moses realized that even though looking to the future was vital for his mission, the people needed hands-on help in the present. Everyone was worried about themselves and their families. So, he began to spend more time meeting one on one with everyone to help each person to work out his or her problems. This was the right thing to do, but not the best method. With thousands of people to see, there was no way he could do it all. This was too burdensome for him to manage alone.

Moses needed a process and structure to accomplish this monumental task. His father-in-law saw how he was exhausting himself trying to do everything for everyone, so he offered him advice. His wise relative recommended that Moses organize the masses into smaller groups, appoint leaders over each group, then a leader over the group leaders, and have the top leaders report to him. If a problem was too difficult for the other leaders to solve, then Moses would step in. Moses took his kinsman's advice."

"Sounds smart," Gage interjected.

"It sure was," Samuel said, nodding. "And things got better for a while. But soon disenchantment set in again. The people needed purpose and structure, but there was more. They needed to understand how to behave; to be shown what was acceptable behavior as they traveled on this exodus together, which could not be the same as their past. The people had gotten out of the foreign land, but the foreign land had not gotten out of them. They needed grace-filled principles to live by from God, instead of the fear-filled rules they had learned in the foreign land. They needed common understanding on how to behave based on their purpose as a people. They needed something consistent to guide their decisions and instruct their behavior rather than having each person do what he or she felt was right in their own mind."

"Yes, clear roles and responsibilities are important," Aaron said.

"Indeed. God called Moses up on a mountain and provided him with some rules to live by. There were ten actually, so we call them the Ten Commandments. These would be the principles of God that Moses taught to the people. They would serve as the common values to live by and lead by. Of course, some people struggled with what felt like directives, and they pushed back. There was much dissension and even mob threats during this time. Along the way, most, but not all, experienced God's hand of protection and realized the value of His principles. They recommitted themselves to their decision to reach their Promised Land."

Samuel nodded to his audience as he wrapped up his lesson. "Amazingly, when they held to these ten core values, the complaining grew quieter and the thankfulness grew louder, and their new culture was born. In the end, those who chose to honor the commandments made it to the Promised Land, but it's important to understand that the journey did not end there. There were still challenges to be met, and they went through the emotions of transition again and again. Change is a constant, and the process of growth requires that we continue to declare endings when needed in order to move forward. The Promised Land changes as we continue our journey of life, and we hope to learn how to get through our wildernesses in a healthy way as a person and a people."

"This is all wonderful and has helped us so much," Cyrus said to Samuel, "but may I ask you one more question. You had called these 'grace-filled principles.' Where does the grace come in?"

"Good question," said Samuel. "The idea of ten commandments sounds pretty unyielding and rule-driven, so where is the grace in that? Those of us who worship our God and have studied His Word know that He would prefer a relationship rather than rules, but the people were fearful and stubborn. The commandments were a way to save the people from going down their self-centered, self-destructive path."

Bahram, who had been listening intently to Samuel, interrupted the explanation. "Your God's approach reminds me of the two signs we saw in the inn a few days ago. We all benefit from knowing what is expected of us and holding people to a standard of excellence, but with people life happens and we need grace. The sign that said, 'Everyone has unseen battles they are fighting, be kind' reminds us that in hard times, showing grace can help people begin to get better and move closer to becoming their best self, but holding on to the truth is important too."

They were stunned for a moment at Bahram's words. Then they chuckled honorably at this simple metaphor of the character of Samuel's God.

It was getting late, so the men expressed their gratitude to Samuel for making the Exodus story come alive. With their journals and minds full of ideas, they stood up to say goodbye and waved as they walked away. The hour seemed too late for extended travel, and since they were still in Jerusalem, they opted to head for the inn instead of setting up camp.

They chatted about the day and were thankful for what they had experienced. Happy and tired, they quickly settled in and enjoyed a good night's rest before continuing their trek towards home.

The next day, a surprising event happened.

CHAPTER TEN

Sounds of the hectic city woke them, and they rose and dressed. After breakfast they began walking through the streets on their long journey back to their kingdom. The area was still bustling as the last of the visiting family members headed back to their homes after their time of celebration. The men soon tired of weaving their way through the shoulder-to-shoulder crowds and looked for a place to get out of the way. They noticed patios nearby where groups of people were sitting and talking together, but they walked a bit farther and found a spot to sit in the courtyard right outside the temple.

Cyrus spoke, "Before we get wrapped up in our travel plans, I wanted to take a moment to talk about what we heard yesterday. Learning about the story of Moses and the people going through the wilderness to their Promised Land was interesting." He gazed at the temple and the people all around, and then back at his friends and asked, "Is there anything you have seen or heard that might help us all be better leaders as Darrius urged us to be?"

"Yes," Gage answered, "the Meal of Remembrance was so

orderly, so systematic, and so filled with tradition. It made a great impression on me."

Bahram added, "And it was really notable that Moses was able to persuade people to take big risks. They probably thought it would be easier to stay where they were, but that happens in a lot of situations we face too. Sometimes you have to talk people into doing things that are good for them."

"I was thinking," Aaron, added reflectively, "I can imagine that the ruler liked 'free labor,' but when you build your kingdom with unjust practices, it's not going to go well for you."

"True," Cyrus said. "Everything you are saying is true. That's why I think this would be good for us to take some time to consider together so we truly understand the principles."

Suddenly everyone's head turned.

Hardy banter and laughter filled the air. It came from a group of older men sitting far away, but inside the court of the temple. The group was large and growing. It had become so large that some stood in the doorway or sat on the window seats. Given their formal dress, the men appeared to be religious leaders who had most likely gathered to discuss important matters. Their jovial behavior seemed out of place.

From within this group, however, a much younger voice rose up. Surprised and curious, Cyrus moved closer to peek through a window and his friends followed. There they saw a boy, about 10 or 12, sitting comfortably in the middle of what they had determined were a group of religious teachers.

The four friends could hear the boy matching wits with the well-trained religious leaders asking insightful questions and sharing ideas that seemed way beyond his years. Passionate conversation about big and small questions were being debated, with the young boy holding his own. He told humorous stories with authority and wisdom. It was as if he was a man of great community standing rather than a boy. What kind of child is this, the friends wondered?

The courtyard filled with more people who obviously had heard about this amazing boy and had come to see for themselves. Very aware that protocol would not permit them to go into the inner court to hear more, Cyrus, Gage, Bahram, and Aaron got up and walked into the crowded street. They continued to talk, as they headed out of the city and towards home.

As they approached the main gate of the city, the sight of a woman in distress interrupted their conversation. She was walking quickly, just ahead of the man who followed her, and others were not far behind.

"Is everything okay?" Cyrus asked, concerned.

"Our son … he was with us here a few days ago," the woman responded. "We left to go home and realized he wasn't in the caravan. We are hurrying back to find him."

"I'm so sorry. Can we help?" Cyrus asked as he paused. Then Bahram said the words he was thinking.

"My dear woman, you look familiar. I believe we have met once before."

"Yes, I think we have," Gage added. "And I think we can help you and your husband find your son."

"We're turning around, my friends," Aaron said, and to the woman, he added, "follow us."

Soon, they were back near the temple. They pointed out the crowded doorway to the woman. She moved closer and could hear the boy speaking with the men in the temple. The woman recognized her son's voice. When she called out to him, he came quickly toward her.

"Son, we were so worried about you," she said.

He answered, "I am sorry for worrying you, but I thought you would know where I would be." His mother had a look of distant amazement on her face, but quickly displayed a mother's practical care and hugged her son tightly.

When she let him go, he turned around, and the four men gasped. There he stood in a white shirt exactly like theirs, but with pearl white buttons. They looked at the mother and she said, "We only let him wear it on special occasions." The boy looked up with questions in his eyes. She said to him, "I'll explain on the way home. Let's go now. Everyone is worried sick and needs to know you are all right."

Bahram was the first to whisper the question, "Wasn't that the shirt the king had us take as a gift to the baby? That had to be over 10 years ago."

Cyrus nodded, "I believe it was."

This boy's presence and the circumstances of their meeting impressed them in a profound way as it had years ago, and each had his own thoughts. "We knew this family was special, but who is he? What kind of child *is* this?"

The men began their journey home yet again, amazed by the extraordinary experiences that had taken place in just a few short days.

Cyrus echoed what they were all thinking, "We have stepped into a lot of different rivers since I first opened that letter and learned the news about Darrius. This journey has brought much change into our lives. As we return home, we have another strategy to develop. Tomorrow I would like for each of you to write down what you have learned about change and transition."

CHAPTER ELEVEN

Cyrus, Aaron, Gage, and Bahram sat around a warm fire relaxing after a breakfast of dried fish, figs, and hard bread. They had spent the night in the cave where Cyrus had camped many years before when he met Darrius for the first time. They all thought this was the perfect place to think and plan. The view across the slow-moving stream, only a few steps outside the cave entrance, made this setting even better.

Sitting near the campfire outside, Cyrus finished the last of his breakfast, then stood and walked into the cave. Aaron followed. Bahram and Gage were still munching on the last few figs when Gage announced, "It's time. We need to record some of the things we've heard and seen. We have talked about this long enough."

Bahram responded, "Get your journal, and we'll go back in and make our notes on the wall." Yet when they walked in, they saw that Cyrus had charcoal in his hand and had already begun writing.

Aaron was examining what Cyrus had drawn on the wall. It was a long line with waves in the center. "Cyrus, tell us about those squiggly lines and what that means," he said.

"I will in a few minutes, but first I'd like to hear what each of you has to say. Would you mind if I start with a few questions so we can proceed in an organized fashion?"

"Amen," said Bahram. "I'm ready to get this done and be on the road to my family. Go ahead, Cyrus."

"Let's start with a little background," Cyrus said. "We began this conversation about change and transition weeks ago as we started our travels together. We shared some very personal experiences. Then we spent time with Darrius and heard his last words, saw his family grieving, experienced a Meal of Remembrance, and heard the Exodus story. Then yesterday once again we encountered that boy full of wisdom beyond his years."

Aaron asked, "May I add something here? Have you noticed that we have planned to stop and do this several times, but distraction after distraction kept getting in the way? But after our encounter with the couple and their son, it's as if a supernatural peace has settled in on us. This feels just like the first time we saw him in Bethlehem where the star had shown so brightly above him."

Everyone was quiet. Their silence sat among them as a collective confirmation of this truth they shared that could not be explained, but only believed.

Cyrus thanked Aaron for his insight as everyone nodded. Then he said, "I'd like each of you to think about these experiences and share any lessons you learned or insights you gained and write it in a few words on the wall with this charcoal. Does that work for everyone?"

"Sure" they shouted in unison, and their voices echoed deep in the cave, again and again.

"It sounds like all the world agrees," said Bahram as everyone laughed. He pointed to the wall. "Anyway, Cy, why don't you lead us on?"

Cyrus stood in front of the wall. "This is the drawing I made when we were listening to Samuel. It depicts crossing the sea and wandering through the wilderness to the Promised Land. I learned that we need to experience an ending, a sea-opening experience, so we can walk away from the past before we can really move through the stages of transition."

He pointed toward the middle of the line. "This wavy line depicts the wave of emotion or stages of feelings we need to go through as we move toward our Promised Land or our next promising step in life, a new beginning so to speak."

"Yes," Bahram interrupted. "It's like when we were talking about our trials on our trip here. Each one of us described how we felt and told each other what we observed about each other's behavior. We each had our own way of getting into, and then through, our wilderness experiences, with a lot of ups and downs like you drew there."

Bahram continued, "Letting go of the past or having an ending is something I never thought about and have certainly never done. I can see now the price I've paid in my relationships. It is easy to let your natural reaction get in the way of getting what you really want." He walked to the wall and wrote:

Personality: Each person responds to change in his or her own way. Allow him or her to tell their story so they can begin to move through the emotions of their transition.

Aaron spoke up, "When we were listening to Samuel, I wrote down the word principles. The Ten Commandments that he talked about seemed to be an important key to their moving forward. This set of values or common principles instructed them on how they needed to behave, and so they worked together instead of letting feelings or biases guide their decisions." He walked to the wall and wrote:

Principles: Shared beliefs help people stay true to their individual and collective purpose and work together during transition.

Gage chimed in, "When I was listening to Samuel, the word that came to me was process. He talked about Moses trying to handle all the problems for each person. I almost went out of my mind imagining that poor guy trying to do it all himself. Finally, Moses decided to set up a structure and process to serve everyone with order and efficiency. You all know I could have told old 'Mo' what to do and saved him all his struggling."

"All right, Gage," said Bahram. "We know you are the master of efficiency, but what did you learn that you want to share with us?"

"Well," said Gage, "My point is…" He walked to the cave wall with charcoal in hand and wrote:

Process: Putting a process and structure in place creates stability and supports progress during the ups and downs of transition.

Cyrus walked to the wall and rewrote their words: Personality, Principles and Process. Then he added his own, Purpose. "Samuel alluded to his belief that once a person or group of people lose their sense of common purpose in something larger than their own desires and wants, confusion and conflict show up. "So, it makes sense to me that knowing your purpose is going to help you get through your transition faster and more effectively, because your personal purpose stays consistent even as you face change."

Purpose: Having a clear hope or important goal means we can act out of a future vision instead of acting as a victim of present or past circumstances.

Cyrus looked over the cave wall and said, "It seems like each of us looked through our individual eyes at the same events and drew different, but valuable observations. Collectively I think we have constructed a map of sorts to help people understand transition and effectively lead themselves and others through the stages when change happens in their lives, career, and family. What do you think?"

"Yes!" they shouted again, just to hear the echo from the cave and have a good laugh.

Cyrus captured all of their work on the wall in his journal.

CHAPTER TWELVE

Even as the four friends worked on their approach to talk about the transition process with their home kingdom, little did they realize, their kingdom was in turmoil. By the end of that day when Cyrus first met Shadan in the king's waiting area, the damage was already underway.

When Shadan came calling and presented credentials from several kingdoms where he had worked, the king was willing to grant him an audience. The meeting had taken place that afternoon, after the king has met with his four trusted advisors.

Shadan had entered the room at a moment when the king felt especially tired and when his cough returned. In this state of ill health, the king feared his weakness and vulnerability, yet he also wondered if this meeting was just a bit too timely.

As the king coughed his way through the discussion, he desperately wanted easy answers to a pressing question: What if he did not survive this bout of illness? He obviously did not want his children to be unprepared. His urgency felt real, and he was ready to respond to the next person who offered a quick solution. That person was Shadan.

With confident swagger, Shadan showed the king credentials of experience in several kingdoms. The king had looked at the list of places he had served, all with kings he knew well. But he noticed one name conspicuously absent on the list, a kingdom now being ruled by a wise and capable queen.

He asked Shadan if he had visited in this particular kingdom, and Shadan had a quick answer. "Ah, yes, I was deeply concerned at the state of their affairs given that the queen is so new to her reign, yet they were clearly not ready for this type of strategy. Perhaps in a few years, as things get worse, they will change their minds. But when you are dealing with people who are so resistant to sound principles …" Shadan shrugged, "The status quo has a strong pull, doesn't it? Well, sometimes they have to realize their error on their own."

The king nodded. That made sense, since people resist good ideas almost as often as they resist bad ones.

The king acknowledged, "We can't teach people what they don't want to learn." But he remained surprised that a new queen who seemed poised to do so well was someone who didn't want to learn.

Days later, when the four friends were still at the beginning of their long journey, Shadan began to implement big changes in the kingdom. His tactics were harsh and severe focusing only on numbers, with total disregard for the impact on people. Soon posters appeared around the kingdom that displayed the profit-at-all-cost centered policies.

◆ ◆ ◆

The 3 New Rules of Work for All Employees

Change happens. Deal with it.
Be loyal. Your manager is always right.
Stay busy and don't waste time asking questions.

Motto: *You must deliver the numbers on time, every time, or you will not have a job.*

◆ ◆ ◆

In the managers' offices and Shadan's training room, his 3 E's were hammered into the leaders' heads and motivated by his reminder: "Comply and be rewarded. Don't comply and be gone."

◆ ◆ ◆

Shadan's 3 E's of Management

1 – Explaining Is Unnecessary
Your employees don't need to understand the reason behind the change. This will only confuse them and make them less productive. It's good to tell people change is coming one time, but limit communication; they won't listen anyway. Quiet any laughter; this is work not play. They need to keep their heads down and keep pushing to the goal. Hold your cards close to the

vest and act like you know best, even if you're not sure. Remind them often: if they can't change fast here, they can change employers fast, like right now. Fear is the best motivator.

2 – Emphasize Vagueness

What the future is going to look like after you implement the change is none of the employee's business. This is the best way to stay in control. Change initiatives need to get off to a fast start and generate a lot of initial confusion, which you can capitalize on to control people. Be as unspecific as you can or, even better, send mixed messages. Don't worry if things get off track. It will keep people busy, and busy is the best thing for everyone during change. Setting up clear roles or any action plan is meaningless during change because, well, it's all going to change anyway. It's all about looking like you are in charge. If you appear weak in any way, people will doubt you and you will have a revolt on your hands. Be confidently evasive, and you will control the game.

3 – Empathy Is Overrated

In any organization, people are overloaded with responsibilities. Listening to your people's concerns about workload is a waste of time and just slows everything down. Stress is good for people. As they say, "When the going gets tough, the tough get going." Don't invest in any extra tools or training during change because that's another distraction. The only thing that matters is producing and hitting the numbers. Of course, people will have family issues; we all do, but tell them to get over it. Work is work, and family is not work and not your concern. Being a counselor is not in your job description. Kindness kills productivity.

Motto: Whoever delivers the numbers on time, every time, wins. There are no other rules.

◆ ◆ ◆

Morale in the kingdom began to plummet. Yet the four friends knew nothing of this. They were about to find out, due to a chance encounter, upon their return to the kingdom, in just a few days.

CHAPTER THIRTEEN

"This trip has been special," Cyrus said to his friends as they prepared for the last leg of their journey, "and I thank you for sharing it with me."

"I don't think we'll forget this experience," Bahram agreed, "and I don't know any other group of friends I'd rather share it with."

"Indeed," Gage said. "I sense that something in what we've learned can be used to help others, a process of sorts."

"Yes," Aaron added, "we're definitely developing a structure that we can build on."

Cyrus concluded, "We'll need to talk to the king about all these ideas that are percolating. But first, let's get home and see our families and then give His Majesty our report."

As Cyrus said these words, he suddenly recalled something the king had said to all of them before they left. He stood and said to his friends, "Do you remember the king mentioning the queen in a nearby kingdom and that it might be good for us to meet and discuss the progress she has made there?"

They all rolled their eyes. They were ready to head home. Weary silence filled the cave. Bahram glanced at Cyrus and said, "I know we're all anxious to get home and this change of plans is not what we wanted, but we do serve at the pleasure of the king. I think we need to honor his request." Gage and Aaron sighed their agreement.

"The queen's kingdom is not far off our route home," Cyrus said. "Can we agree to stop there and see if she is willing to meet with us? If we are not welcomed, we will move on towards home?" The men nodded.

"Well let's go," Gage said. "It looks like it could take two extra days to get there, but I remember when we were traveling from home, I saw another path that crossed over towards the queen's territory. It may be a quicker route."

The men loaded their donkeys quickly and headed for their new destination at a fast pace. There wasn't much conversation among the four as they rode along. They were all anxious to get this over, each one silently hoping the queen would not be there or she would refuse to talk to them, so they could get on home. But because of Gage's new travel route and their hard riding, they arrived at the gate to the queen's kingdom near sunset that very day.

The guard at the large city gate stopped them and asked in a stern voice, "Who are you, and what is your reason to be coming to our kingdom?" As he looked upon the travelers with suspicion, Cyrus explained their goal, and then he apologized for not having their king send word ahead of time. He told the guard they would understand if the queen could not see them.

Cyrus noticed the guard's demeanor soften. Then he said, "My name is Cyrus. What is yours?"

"Taye," the guard answered.

"Taye, we know it is very late, and I wouldn't want to interrupt Her Majesty this evening, but I would appreciate it if you would convey to her our request that we spend an hour with her tomorrow morning."

Cyrus's unassuming approach worked and the guard said, "I would be happy to get your request to Her Majesty and send word back to you in the morning if she is available."

Cyrus was taken aback by the guard's dramatic change of attitude and said, "Thank you for your help. When we first arrived, I wasn't so sure we had much of a chance to even get inside the gate."

The guard said, "Let me explain the reason for my brashness. Not long ago I was on guard duty, and a pushy, loudmouth fellow showed up at the gate. He insisted that he needed to see our queen. He pushed past me and got to my supervisor and started name-dropping about important people he knew and demanded that he be seen by the queen. Somehow this scoundrel got in to see Her Majesty, but he didn't stay long. The queen ran him out of town with his tail between his legs." He laughed.

The guard went on, "So you can see why I reacted to your request the way I did. Then you showed some humility and kindness, and I knew I was dealing with a different type of person."

The travelers listened to this unexpected treasure of hearing the guard's viewpoint. He went on to say, "I don't know why I'm telling you this, but my mother passed away not long ago, and I guess I'm still dealing with that loss." He shrugged.

The four men looked at each other. Then Aaron said, "Taye, can I show you something that might help? Aaron told him about change, endings and the process of transition. Then he drew the "wave of emotions" that occur when change happens. He asked Taye where he felt like he was in this picture. Aaron concluded, "Each of our personalities move through the emotions of transition in our own way."

Taye smiled and said, "Now I understand that what I'm going through is natural for everyone. Thank you so much for opening my eyes. Maybe I can help my brothers understand how to heal their grief." He looked up to the evening sky and said, "It is dark now and I need to help you get settled for the night."

The guard wrote a referral note and gave them the name of the livery stable manager and the owner of the nearby lodge to arrange for their animals' care and their own lodging for the night. The four of them thanked him sincerely. They were exhausted, so after a short dinner, they headed for their rooms. As they lay in their beds, each wondered about the meeting with the queen the next day. Soon their heavy eyes closed and they were fast asleep.

CHAPTER FOURTEEN

The next morning, they were having coffee in the main gathering area when they heard some commotion and looked up. There stood a palace guard in full armor. "Who is Cyrus?" he asked. Cyrus stood. "Her Majesty the Queen has accepted your request and would like to meet with you and your men within the hour. I will wait here to give you time to prepare yourselves and then escort all of you to the palace."

"We are ready now," Cyrus said. They grabbed their journals from the table and followed the guard. He seated them in the waiting area where they discussed questions they would ask the queen. A loud bell rang, and they stood and were escorted by a palace official into the throne room where they saw the queen. They bowed with respect yet were surprised when the queen stepped from her throne and said, "Please sit here with me at the table."

Once seated, the queen said, "I seldom meet with unannounced visitors, but I know and admire the king you serve, plus I heard about the kindness you showed to Taye. I was intrigued and wanted to meet you. Please tell me why you have come."

Cyrus began, "We come at the request of our king who has heard much about the wonderful things you have achieved in your kingdom. He asked us to see if you would share some of your philosophies and concepts that we might apply to make our kingdom healthy and more productive. The reason he did not send his request beforehand is because we have been on a long journey, and, as we were headed home, it was convenient for us to stop here with the hope that we might gain an audience with you. We are thankful you were gracious enough to do so."

The queen, a very direct and candid person, said, "My father died two years ago after a lengthy illness, and I ascended to the throne. Before he passed away, he sat with me and shared his vision for the kingdom and asked me to write down my vision for the future of the kingdom. My father always said, 'A leader must have clear goals to achieve and provide a culture for pursuing the kingdom's vision.' He wanted me to understand that the atmosphere that motivates people to achieve the goals is also important. So, I wrote my goals and vision. Some parts were similar to my father's, other parts were my own." She took a long breath.

"It took me a year after he passed away to get over his death and share my vision with the palace officials and then with all the people. As you would imagine, I proposed some big goals which came with significant changes. Well, you know how people are about change. Some were fully on board. Some were angry. Many were just shocked. Never having been the leader before, I was not prepared for the emotional reactions of those around me to my new initiatives. I didn't know what to do. But I remembered what my father said: 'To lead your people walk behind them.' That's what I did. We held small group meetings and listened to the people in our kingdom talk about the future, and we came up with ways we could move forward together.

"About that time this con artist showed up. He was arrogant and proud, but he was confident and convincing about his principles and process for moving people through change 'fast and efficiently,' as he would say. But when he explained his autocratic, fear-based, numbers-driven approach, I thought of my people as individuals, how they would react, and how I would feel if I were in their shoes. I knew this guy had the potential to cause great damage to our culture, and I sent him away almost as soon as he finished his opening proposal."

The men had many questions, but the queen did not have time that day to answer any of them. She had a full day of responsibilities, but as she said goodbye, she opened the door to a future visit. "I'd like to hear about your journey and give you time to learn about some of the things we're doing here," she said.

They bowed and said goodbye. They left the palace and rushed to the livery stable, anxious to get on the road and talk about their conversation with the queen.

CHAPTER FIFTEEN

As they were loading their packs on their donkeys, a weary traveler arrived at the stable to drop off his pack animals. Cyrus saw him and thought he had met him before.

"Hello," Cyrus said in a friendly greeting. The man seemed preoccupied and totally in his own world.

"Sir?" Cyrus spoke again, as he puzzled over the familiarity of the man's face.

"Oh, hello," the stranger finally said. Tired and worn down, he dropped the bag he had been carrying and used it as a stool.

Cyrus continued, "I must ask you, have we met? You look familiar."

The man shrugged as he propped his head on a bent elbow.

Cyrus said, "Wait, did I meet you once in Jerusalem? My friend Darrius had advised me to go around to the different groups that gathered in town to learn more about the work people did."

"Yes, I was probably there." He looked at Cyrus. "I guess you seem familiar. I'm sorry. I'm a little distracted."

Bahram spoke, if only to state the obvious. "If you'll pardon my saying so, sir, you seem to be discouraged."

"Oh, you have no idea. I had been working with a business associate of mine, a former business associate, that is. He had this new venture where he was selling companies on how he could help them grow quickly and make change happen fast."

Aaron asked, "And it was too good to be true?"

"Very! He said he had it all figured out. He just needed a little investment money to turn things around for my company. I guess I wanted to believe him, but it was an expensive lesson. I lost a lot of money and I almost lost my company. So, I'm on the road a lot trying to build it back up. My shortcut turned into a really long delay."

"I'm sorry to hear that," Cyrus said sympathetically. "We've been talking a lot about change on our journey. You have reminded us of how important it is to have a good transition system in place. We plan to teach this strategy as soon as we get it ready."

"So, what happened to that man?" Gage asked.

"After he did a lot of damage with companies, he switched to government. He's been implementing his system in several kingdoms. Well, except for this one. When he met the queen, she immediately anticipated the damage his process could do. She sent him packing quickly. Frankly, that's why I'm here. This kingdom still has a lot of opportunity, whereas others have suffered, especially if they listened to my former business associate. After he was run out of this kingdom, he was quickly on to the next victim."

"Who was that?" Aaron asked.

"Well, there's this king who is in declining health, so he wanted to prepare his kingdom for his inevitable departure, shall we say. He just handed the whole thing over to Shadan. He basically said, 'Just get it done.' And let me tell you, when Shadan got that free rein, so to speak, that reign became doomed."

Cyrus felt a cold sweat. "Oh, no ...," he said with an ominous tone.

The man pulled out a jug. "I better get some water. I'll have to be back on the road soon. Good luck to you fellows. When you do start teaching your strategy, be sure to tell them to do the work the right way. This guy kept saying things like, 'Make change happen fast. Hitting the numbers on time, every time, is all that matters.'" The traveler stood and shook his head with deep regret. "Don't get involved with people like Shadan."

By now Cyrus's heart was pounding. "We need to go. We need to get home now."

The others looked to Cyrus and could clearly see his concern, even horror. They quickly said goodbye to the stranger and began their journey. On the way, Cyrus told them about a man he'd once met named Shadan, someone who talked a fast game that led to big losses.

"Do you think our king is the king he is referring to?" Gage asked with concern.

"Right before we left, I spoke to him in the king's waiting area. I was sure our king would be too smart for any of his shenanigans, but maybe his poor health affected his decision-making." The men picked up their speed.

CHAPTER SIXTEEN

It was twilight when they arrived in their own kingdom, and they were understandably eager to end their travels and see their families. Yet when they entered the gates, they saw an immediate commotion. A crowd had gathered, and the returning men could hear high-pitched voices of complaint and frustration.

Cyrus could see stress, anxiety, and even tears on their faces. "Hello," he said as the crowd turned in his direction. He recognized several of the people, and one of the women quickly spoke. "Oh, Cyrus, we're glad you're home. Surely the king will listen to you."

"What's the matter?" Cyrus asked. "What has happened?"

"The king has made a lot of changes in the last few weeks, and it's been just miserable," she said. "Morale on my team has plummeted. Everybody's nervous and wondering where this is headed."

A man in the crowd said, "All our jobs have been changed to fit a master restructuring plan the king approved. The color buttons don't matter anymore. Production is the only thing that matters."

Another man cleared his throat, and the crowd grew quiet as if following his cue. "There'd been a lot of rumors that jobs were going to be cut," he said in a halting voice. "I tried to pretend what I heard were just rumors and should be ignored, but then I got called into my supervisor's office and he said, 'It's not personal.'"

The man blinked back tears. "I may not be the smartest person in the company, but I know that you shouldn't say anything like 'It's not personal' to a man who isn't sure how he's going to feed his family or keep a roof over his head. You ought to treat people with respect, even if they don't get to keep their job."

Cyrus was deeply moved. "I'm so sorry," he said.

"And he's just the first of it," another man said. "There are rumors that a lot more of us are on the chopping block, but who really knows? No one's telling us what's going on or what's going to happen next."

A woman's voice spoke up and Cyrus turned toward a faithful kingdom employee that he had admired and respected. "We hear all kinds of things. The loudest voices are the ones that get heard, and we don't even know if they know what they're talking about. In the fear and confusion, there's a big void, and it gets filled up with whatever anyone wants to imagine, and it's usually the worst-case scenarios."

The man next to her nodded and said, "I may not know what's going on, but I know this much. The rumors and fear and confusion have spread throughout our kingdom like a wildfire, and this situation has consumed our spirits and extinguished the life-giving culture we had come to cherish."

The crowd grew silent at his summation. Cyrus touched his shoulder and said, "We will do what we can to talk to the king and find out how we can help." Then he turned to his three friends as they looked to each other and said one word, "Shadan."

Bahram tried to soothe the crowd. "We understand that some difficult changes have been put into place. And you're right, the king usually does listen to Cyrus, and we'll help Cyrus speak your concerns."

"We will try to talk to the king first thing tomorrow. Don't lose hope," Gage added.

"This is important to us, too," Aaron echoed. "We don't want to see the good that has been built in our kingdom torn down either. We'll do what we can."

The crowd settled down, and as they dispersed, the four weary travelers began saying their goodbyes to each other. "Let's go to see our families and spend time with them," Aaron said. "We'll meet at the palace in the morning."

They each hugged at the end of this emotional, pivotal journey, even as they suspected a new one was just beginning.

The next day, they met at the palace, and the king soon welcomed them into his chambers. He looked thinner and weaker, but his voice came out stronger than expected.

"Gentlemen," the king said, "seeing you is like a breath of fresh air. My health has been poor in recent weeks, yet I believe I am turning the corner. The medicine I have been taking has been helping. I'm starting to feel like myself again, and I am so glad that you are some of the first people I get to see now that I feel better. Tell me please about your travels and about dear Darrius."

They sat around the king's conference table as they told him of their long journey and especially what they learned about change and transition. The king listened intently, and then he spoke.

"My friends, it seems I have made a mistake, a big one. I have been swayed by an untrustworthy voice that told me things

I wanted to hear, and in my illness, I was vulnerable enough to listen. As a result, I have allowed problems to be created in the kingdom instead of seeing that they were solved. These problems have grown and festered, when I had hoped they would resolve under these strategies Shadan implemented."

The king signaled to an aide. "Bring me the posters." He laid the long sheet on the table and explained to the four gentlemen, "Here are the three principles of change that Shadan used to guide us. This is the poster that had been displayed in our planning room at the palace as well as in other rooms where Shadan taught his management theory to our leaders and managers. Here is the poster he has plastered in every workplace for all employees to see."

They read Shadan's 3 E's of Management – Explaining is unnecessary. Emphasize vagueness. Empathy is overrated. Then the employee mandates: Change happens - deal with it; Be loyal - Your manager is always right; Stay busy and don't waste time asking questions.

The four men were shocked, but in a respectful voice, Cyrus said, "Sire, Darrius told us that anyone can make a change, but it takes a leader to lead a transition. Shadan pushed for a dramatic change in managing the kingdom. It did not work because he didn't know the difference between change and transition."

The king nodded solemnly. "As you have described the process to me, I realize that we need a clear ending for the problem I created." He called out to the chief of guards, "Go get Shadan now and bring him to me." Then the king turned to his chief administrator, "Call for a meeting of all the key leaders in my kingdom this afternoon at sunset in the large meeting hall."

He faced Cyrus, Bahram, Gage, and Aaron, "I intend to send a strong message that we are ending the old way now and beginning our road to peace and prosperity again. I need you to be prepared to share an overview of what you have learned about transition at this meeting today." They nodded in unison.

CHAPTER SEVENTEEN

It was late afternoon, and all were gathered in the large meeting room in the palace. There was a platform at the far end of the room. On one side stood Shadan. His head was bowed in shame, with one guard on his right arm, one on his left arm, and one behind him. The king stood on the other side of the stage beside a table with a basin of water and a towel.

"Thank you for being here on such short notice," the king said. "This is an urgent matter. As you all know, I have made a grave mistake. A few weeks ago, I took the advice of Shadan on how to improve our kingdom and make change happen fast. The actions he recommended, and I took, were wrong and almost destroyed the wonderful culture we have created over the years."

After talking with Cyrus, Aaron, Bahram, and Gage about change and transition and the steps in the process, I now realize my good intentions were a mistake. I also learned that having a clear ending of this current situation is required so we can move forward to our good way of life again."

The king reached over to the basin of water and dipped his hands in and brought them up. As he dried his large hands on the towel, he said, "Let it be known that our past is past." He then turned to the guards. "Escort Shadan out of our kingdom through the main gates for all the people to see. I want to send a message to the people that we are ending Shadan's plans and beginning anew. Collect all the posters of Shadan's three rules and burn them in the public square for all to see."

Turning to the crowd, the king continued, "When you leave, please tell all those who report to you about today's meeting and that we have washed our hands of the past. To help you understand why I did what I did today, Cyrus will speak." He looked to the guards nearing the exit and said, "Wait. I want Shadan to hear this message as well so that he can understand how he led us astray."

Cyrus stood in front of the crowd, even as he avoided making eye contact with Shadan. He well remembered how easy it is to be taken in by the promise of quick solutions. Extending a hand toward Aaron, Bahram, and Gage, he said, "We learned valuable lessons during our recent journey, and we are grateful to have the opportunity to share them with our kingdom." He then spoke of their experiences and what they had learned about the differences between change and transition. He explained the brutal policies of the pharaoh, drew his illustration of the events of the Exodus, the ending at the sea, wandering in the wilderness, and how grace makes it all work.

Though there were a few questions among the attendees, it was clear to Cyrus that the people in the room understood the value of this process.

The king said, "Thank you, Cyrus, and let me express my gratitude to Bahram, Gage, and Aaron as well." Then he added, "Bring Shadan here." Shadan walked up with the guards, though he kept his head down. "Do you have anything you would like to say?" asked the king.

Shadan looked up and managed to restore his cocky manner long enough to try to talk the king into believing in him again. "Sire, you are so wise to listen to Cyrus. And you are right. My strategy needed some fine-tuning. What Cyrus has presented is a brilliant strategy that will tie together nicely with what I have installed in your kingdom. I would welcome the chance to receive your grace and work with Cyrus on his new plan."

The king nodded solemnly. "You will receive my grace, Shadan. I will allow you to live, and not to be stoned to death, as I am sure many of my suffering people would rush to do to you, if given half a chance. I will not keep you imprisoned and at the mercy of the guards whose pay you suggested be cut in half. But you will lose your treasure and most importantly you will lose your reputation for generations to come. For now, when people speak of you in this kingdom, it won't be unlike how they speak of the pharaoh in that long-ago kingdom. For how people lead through transition is how they are ultimately remembered."

Then the king turned to the men in front of him. "Cyrus, Aaron, Bahram, and Gage, I am grateful for your loyal service. I believe your journey and the wisdom you gained is something that should be shared with others in our kingdom. I would like for you to formalize what you've learned, develop specific tools, and begin teaching this philosophy to the leaders in our kingdom."

"Yes, Sire," they said in one voice.

"You will be the ones who share the wisdom of transition with our beloved kingdom," the king concluded. So, roll up your sleeves and get to work." With that, he stood and left the room as the four men and the crowd of leaders rose to their feet.

CHAPTER EIGHTEEN

The men exhaled deeply as they tried to sort through the meeting they'd just been through.

Cyrus said, "Well, we've been given another important responsibility. Fortunately, we've already laid the groundwork for where we want to go."

"Yeah, but we better get this on a schedule," Gage added. "We need timelines."

Bahram laughed, "Don't worry, Gage. We'll make sure there's plenty of structure for you." Gage smiled sheepishly but appreciatively, realizing it was nice to be recognized for the strengths he brought to the table.

The men immediately gathered in a smaller room and began to refine their transition strategy based on Personality, Principles, Process, and Purpose. Cyrus returned to the drawing they had begun in the cave, and that he had recorded in his journal.

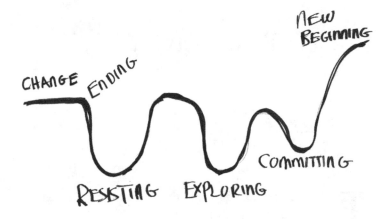

"This looks pretty good," said Gage, "but it needs to be cleaned up some." Aaron rolled his eyes as he said lightheartedly, "We'll get it perfectly perfect later. It's perfectly good for now."

Before Aaron and Gage could get into an argument, Bahram stepped in. "This looks very good, but there seems to be something missing. I can't put my finger on it, but I think it needs a personal touch we may have overlooked. What do you say, Cyrus?"

"Funny you should ask," Cyrus said. "A few days ago, I was thinking about Darrius's profound words about how any change, positive or negative, could elicit the same transition emotions. I recalled the emotional ups and downs Heather and I experienced as we got married and began our new lives together. Then there was the next joyful life-changing event, the birth of our first child, our son Darrius.

"I'm sure you sketched that out somewhere," said Bahram with a smirk. Cyrus sighed, and then turned to another page in his journal. They moved in closer to look at Cyrus's notes.

◆ ◆ ◆

Cyrus's Journal Page

Change event: Marriage and Honeymoon
Transition stages: shock of having to share things with another person > conflict deciding what our new roles were > exploring new ways of being > counting our blessings and remembering that our marriage commitment meant forever > enjoying a new beginning as a couple

Change event: Birth of Son and Ending of Our Simple Life
Transition stages: Shock that we were parents > Upset because things weren't the same > resisting our new roles and finally agreeing who had what job in our new family world > exploring ways to parent > Being thankful again for all we had > Commitment to one another and this new world of family.

◆ ◆ ◆

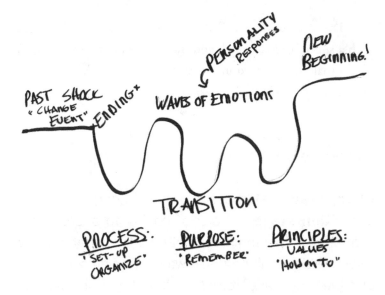

"As you may have guessed, after we had our conversations on the ride in, I made some notes as well," Cyrus said. The group smiled. "I wrote down what I heard about how each of you reacted to the surprise and changes. Please realize that this is not faultfinding, but remember Darrius told us when a person is hit by an unexpected change, he or she, in his words, 'can go out of their right mind.' They are not their best self for a while. Shock reaction is a good way to look at this."

The men looked at what Cyrus had written.

He also noted that a person's initial change response is based on each person's natural personality style. He listed their names. Beside each name he wrote his observation of each one's initial reaction to change.

Aaron – Needlessly busy, detached, showing little empathy
Bahram – Argumentative, unfocused or dominating

Gage – Withdrawn, over-controlling or resistant
Cyrus – Pessimistic, too idealistic or indecisive

"I know that this is more than you expected me to say today, but what do you think?" Cyrus asked.

Aaron said in a good-natured tone, "Looks like you've had too much time on your hands, Cyrus." Then he slapped him on the back and laughed, "but seriously it makes sense to me. How about the rest of you?"

Gage's and Bahram's certain look conveyed their buy-in. Then Gage said, "I do need to process this a little more, as you see there." He looked at the notes, raised one eyebrow, smiled and said, "I don't know what we would do without you and your need to notice. Thank you."

But by the look in Cyrus's eyes, everyone knew there was more to come.

"One more question," Cyrus, said. "As we look at this drawing and think about all we have seen and heard, what would each of you say is the one thing we need to remember if we want to be effective in leading people through transition to their promised land, or a new beginning when change hits them?"

Silence. Each man looked at the other and then looked down.

Cyrus said, "Well, I'll go first. Transition is easier once you know your purpose. Your purpose doesn't change but evolves. The work that we did earlier to help people find their career purpose still applies, but this is to help them with the next step, and the next, and the next … because change is always going to happen."

"Agreed," Aaron said, "and now I've thought of something. You all know that I tend to try to get to the simplest answer as fast as I can. Sometimes I move too fast and just go with an idea that may be way off base, but I have an answer. This time I hope I have this right." He paused in a non-Aaron-like way and said, "My answer for the best way to help people get through a transition is: listen and ask questions that lead them forward to their next step." Everyone nodded in agreement.

Gage said, "That's what Darrius told us on his death bed. Great leaders are great listeners. I think he knew we would figure the question part out, but questions don't matter if you aren't listening."

Bahram remembered, "Yes, and we watched that young boy in the temple influencing men five times his age by asking questions and listening intently."

Cyrus recalled the teacher who built his confidence to counsel others at the funeral with a series of interpretive questions, and he wrote on the wall: Ask thoughtful questions, listen, and help them take a step forward to help one another. Suddenly Cyrus recalled the rolled parchment the teacher had handed him after the funeral. But he didn't want to interrupt the flow of this exchange, so he made a mental note to look at the document later that day.

Then Gage spoke, "I know all of these ideas and tools are good and useful. But none of this will ever be effective if they are not done in a caring manner. I haven't forgotten that sign at the inn: 'Everyone has unseen battles they are fighting. Be kind!' I think that has to be the foundation of all we do."

There was a collective silence in the room. They had almost let the most important element they had learned slip by. They smiled and everyone gave Gage a pat on the back.

CHAPTER NINETEEN

Aaron said, "Sounds like we've got a lot of work to do, though. Like the king said, we better 'roll up our sleeves.'"

"You know," Cyrus, said thoughtfully, "I keep hearing that phrase. And I've got an idea."

He turned to a clean page in his journal and sketched three shirts. "What if we go back to a shirt as our metaphor, but this time think about the sleeves instead of the buttons?"

The guys watched as he drew. "So, in the first stage of transition, sleeves are full length," Cyrus said. This symbolizes the shock of the change event, and how we naturally resist the change that is taking place and keep our sleeves as they are for a while. In the second stage, we've warmed up to the idea a little bit, so we roll up our sleeves more. We're willing to hear and learn more during this time of exploration. But after that, we go all in. We're committing to the change, and we're thankful. That's the next stage. We roll our sleeves up over the elbow and we get to work."

Bahram nodded and said, "So, transition is three stages: resisting, exploring, and committing?"

"Yes," Cyrus said, "after the first step—the ending event."

"And each stage leads us through the process." Gage added.

"Then we roll up our sleeves to indicate where we are in the process," Aaron concluded.

"Exactly," Cyrus said with a smile, but with a lingering question in the back of his mind.

As the men prepared to share these transition tools with the kingdom's leaders, Cyrus knew the first person he wanted to teach. "Rafiq!" He called to his neighbor one afternoon a few days later.

"Cyrus, welcome home!" Rafiq responded. "It's so good to see you again. I hope your journey was fruitful."

"Indeed, it was," Cyrus said, "and I've thought quite often about our last conversation before I left on my journey."

"Really?" Rafiq said with surprise.

"Yes, I apologize for not listening to you more closely. You were expressing a serious concern about how to transition in your career. I've got some tools now that I believe will help you with that."

He took out his journal and said, "Let me show you something." Cyrus drew a wave of transition just like the squiggly lines he had drawn on the cave wall.

"This represents what we all go through when we experience change and transition," Cyrus said. "Change is the event, the thing that happens. Transition is what we go through, and that involves an ending and grief and some significant emotional stages. So, tell me about the feelings you experienced and where you are now."

Rafiq's face moved from curiosity to relief as he began to talk about how this good opportunity he'd been given had actually been more difficult to get through than he would have expected.

"Now I understand that what I went through was natural and that I will likely deal with this again in my life," Rafiq said. "I'm really happy about my promotion, and I surely do not want to make mistakes in this big opportunity. I would appreciate more of your insight in how to make this a good transition."

"We will go through this process together," Cyrus assured him. "So, get ready to roll up your sleeves and get to work."

As Cyrus and his friends began teaching the principles of change and transition to people in the kingdom, he continued to use the metaphor of "rolling up your sleeves" and found it gave people an easy way to show how they were doing when dealing with a major change. Instead of saying, "I'm in the stage of resisting or grieving," they would say, "My sleeves are all the way down today." Or, instead of "I'm in the stage of exploring," they might say, "My sleeves are rolled up one more turn today." Everyone knew what rolling up your sleeves all the way meant. "I'm 100% back!" The shirtsleeve symbolism even made it easier for men to talk about how they were really feeling.

However, Cyrus observed two behaviors or responses that concerned him as he taught the *roll up your sleeves* concept. One response was when someone who had just experienced a great loss would immediately say, "I'm fine," and they rolled their sleeves all the way up and got back to work. They didn't realize that they needed to experience their emotions to really get back to 100%, or those emotions like anger, sadness or depression would show up at the most inappropriate times. His greatest challenge was to get people to realize that it was best to start with their sleeves down and go through the various processes of emotional ups and downs. But he learned that each person had his or her own path that helped them get through their own wilderness to a new beginning. Some people chose a rocky up-hill path and had to roll their sleeves up and down several times as they moved forward and back in the transition process. But most would find their way to becoming healthy again.

The second concern was with those who didn't want to roll up their sleeves at all, but instead found too much comfort in the resisting, grieving, and denying. These were often the most challenging people to help. He always went back and asked questions that helped people decide to take their next step. By listening to their story, he found he was able to guide most people to get through their wilderness and back to healthy living and leading again.

As Cyrus and his friends fine-tuned this process, a question still lingered in Cyrus' mind. Then it hit him. He said, "Now I know what is bothering me! In this drawing the waves are smooth, which seems to imply there is steady movement from one stage to the next. We all know that is not the way it is for everyone. The way I react to change is different than how each of you react."

"We agree," they said.

"Remember the first drawing I made when we were just beginning our journey? We were talking about crossing a river with big waves and the fears we had about that, so I made that wave drawing." He opened his journal and showed them the sketch. They remembered and all nodded.

"Real waves crest and curve back the way emotions often turn back a bit before they move forward in each stage. We need to let people know to expect this swaying of emotions. Tell them that it is natural to experience this feeling of unsteadiness. Then ..."

He stopped mid-thought, searching for the right words, and began again. "What if we let each person draw a diagram of how their wave of transition felt to them?"

With a creative gleam in his eye, Cyrus placed a large piece of parchment on the wall. "Let's try that idea and see how it works for us. I'll go first. I recall that I move through feelings which are indirect and withdrawn and might look like this." Sketching on the wall, Cyrus drew a series of smooth waves.

Aaron said, "I'd say my waves would be really tall and steep."

Bahram walked up to draw his waves and said, "I suppose my waves might be similar to Aaron's, but not quite as dramatic."

Gage was last. He slowly sketched waves that looked like a calm sea, with a storm brewing, and said, "I wanted to make my sketch look like Cyrus's, but then I realized I will never be that kind of smooth and steady guy." They all laughed.

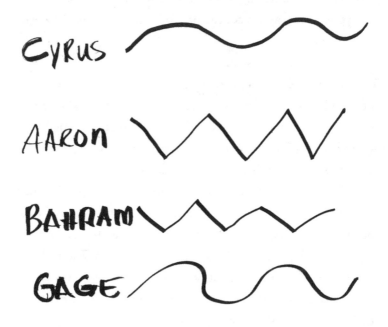

Cyrus said, "I noticed none of us showed our waves crashing, but we know that can sometimes happen to people."

"Yes" the others agreed as Gage added, "I think we learned for this journey, as well as our first trip, that crashes happen more often when you try to handle your waves of transition by yourself and you forget about praying."

Bahram said, "Yes, two are better than one, and as Gage reminded us, we need to kneel more often. Prayer is so simple to do, but so easy to forget."

Cyrus asked, "What do each of you think?

In a sign of spontaneous unity Aaron, Gage, and Bahram reached down and rolled up their sleeves. Cyrus did the same. And they laughed.

Over the next few days, Cyrus documented all the things they had learned and organized a presentation to share with the king.

The following week, their journey concluded in the place it had begun. The king called to convene the four leaders to meet with him at his royal table. They arrived early to set up. When the king walked in, they stood in honor, then he happily greeted them. Then they sat. The king looked up and saw a new poster hanging on the wall in the spot where Shadan's poster had been. He read. They sat in silence.

◆ ◆ ◆

Roll-up Your Sleeves
Ten Observations & One Unshakable Truth

1. **Change is not the same as transition**. Change is an event. Transition is the emotional stages people go through when change happens.

2. **Personality matters**. Every person has a unique way he or she reacts and works through transition. How and when a person rolls up their sleeves and regains their purposeful place is on their clock, not yours.

3. **Role clarity counts.** People are structure-seeking beings. When change hits, each person needs to talk about his or her role and how the change will affect them and the ones they love personally.

4. **Principles set the pace.** Clarity of personal values and shared values guide effective behavior and help set a pace so people can move steadily forward and even grow through their wilderness experience.

5. **Purpose is power**. When people know the *why* behind a change and can see a promised land, both collectively and individually, they can get through transition easier. Without vision or purpose, people tend to go back to their safe endings, no matter how painful those past circumstances were.

6. **Process matters**. Show people a simple model so they can identify where they are in their transition process and progress. Listen and guide them with questions to take ownership of their next step.

7. **Endings let us begin again.** Acknowledgement and acceptance that the past is behind you and that the future is in front of you is worth working through, because it creates forward momentum. Momentum is a wonderful thing.

8. **Seasons come and go**. Life is a series of transitions in which we decide to either loathe the change or learn to love yourself more and serve others willingly. Helping another person get through their struggles is the best way to get through yours.

9. **Self-counseling doesn't work.** When change hits, we become our worst counselor. Instead, share your story with a trusted friend who will listen and not try to fix you. If you go alone, you will go too fast and crash. If you go together, you will go farther and heal. (see #8)

10. **Pray first:** Before life gives you more than you can stand, kneel! The more you kneel along the way, the easier you'll stand the test today.

One Unshakable Truth

Everyone has unseen battles they are fighting. Be kind!

◆ ◆ ◆

When the king finished reading, he smiled and said, "Well done." Then he hesitated and said, "I'd like to suggest one more thing. Yes, the one unshakeable truth of being kind is vital, but speaking truth is just as important. If you men agree, how can that be included?"

Cyrus walked up to the poster, he marked through the title and scribbled:

◆ ◆ ◆

Kind Truth
Everyone has unseen battles they are fighting; be kind and speak truth.

◆ ◆ ◆

There was a collective nod and they all laughed in agreement.

After thanking the king for his wisdom, they reviewed the transition models and relived their shared journey over the past year. The king asked how the training was going with the other people, and Cyrus showed him some of the tools and outlines they were using. The king seemed pleased.

They all stood to leave and the king said, "There is one thing that I need all of you to begin thinking about." Then the door cracked open, and the messenger said, "Sire, this is urgent."

"I apologize. I must go, but we will talk about this matter soon," said the king and then he walked away.

The men look at each other with concern. Then Bahram said, "I think we remember hearing these same words as we walked away from our king's table about a year ago." He grinned. "So check your sleeves, and let's move on." They nodded, and with a sense of optimism slightly restored, they all said goodbye.

Each took a different path home.

You can find practical resources, as well as a take the My Change Management Style quiz on the book website www.rollupsleeves.com Look for the next book in the White Shirt Series coming in 2021.

ACKNOWLEDGMENTS

Many thanks to...

Patricia Tate, my wife and faithful prayer warrior, who uplifts me when I get discouraged with her beautiful bright eyes, loving smile and warm touch, and never stops telling me this is the best book I've ever written.

Bradley, my son, for his steadfast support and insight on healing productivity.

Norman Jetmundsen, Jr., a friend and fellow author and the one who opened the door for me to meet my agent.

Bruce Barbour, my agent, who guided me to little improvements that made a huge difference in this book and again pushed the second book in front of David Hancock, CEO of Morgan James Publishing, who also liked this book a good bit.

Minnie Lamberth, my copywriter and friend, who applied her amazing craft to again mold my vision into a storyline, caught edits everyone else missed and happily took care of many publishing details above and beyond her assigned mission.

A few loyal fans and good friends who graciously offered endorsements and gave time out of their busy lives to help me in many ways: Cliff Eslinger, Elizabeth Jeffries, Pete and Gloria Russell, Robert Russell, Michael Wilson, Bob Seybert, Steve Briggs, Vic Slay, Elliot Colebeck, and all the members of the Sunrise Rotary Club of Birmingham.

My wonderful clients and leaders of amazing organizations who have allowed me to learn about managing change and transition right beside you and your teams: Michael Hasting, Tom Stackhouse, Julie Young, Jennifer Blackmon, Chuck Billings, Jimmy Gray, Jerome Johnston, Tim Martin, Kelly Hutsuffler, Burt Hughes, Micah Andrews, Leslie Freeman, Renée Anne Casillas, Michelle and Bill Hientz, Peter Tilley, Tony Cooper, Anthony Cooper, Suzanne Owens, Chip E. Jakins III, Ed Short, Kim Carter, Mark Parker, Andrew Edwards, Karen Moore, Mark Ingram, Alan Schott, Steve Irwin, Jody Taylor, Briana Coleman, Joe Mead, Jim Mead, Becky White, Ty Kicklighter, and Glenn Bell.

To my new friends in the podcasting world: Tom Schwab and Terri Shrader at Interview Valet who helped me get started and the hosts who graciously invited me on their podcasts this year: Nick Murphy – Transform U podcast; Mario Porreca – 10-minute Mindset; Wally Carmichael – Men of Abundance; Justin and Danielle Williams – Legendary Marriage; Dominic Lawson – Startup Life; Dr. Joey Faucette – Faith Positive Radio; Jeff Altman – Job Search Radio; Mary Lou Kayser – Play Your Position; Andi Simon – On the Brink; Jeff Smith – Vroom Vroom Veer; Don Hutchinson – Discover Your Talent; Sheuel Septimus – Love Your 9 to 5; Brent Tieri – Life Outside the Hustle; and Jason Brooks – LeaderThrive.

RESOURCES FOR FURTHER READING ON CHANGE AND TRANSITION

Managing Transitions by William Bridges and Susan Bridges
First published in 1992, this is an essential guide for leaders who are navigating transitions and change within any organization. It is also a handbook in life for dealing with endings, new beginnings, and the disruptive "neutral zone" in between. The 25th anniversary edition, released in 2017, reintroduces the work of the late William Bridges to a new generation.

The Truth about Employee Engagement by Patrick Lencioni
Released in 2019, Patrick Lencioni takes on the universal problem of job dissatisfaction and stress. The book presents managers with a practical, new approach for engaging employees in order to maximize their potential in a changing workplace.

That's Not How We Do It Here by John Kotter and Holger Rathgeber
This book told in parable form distills John Kotter's decades of experience and award-winning research to reveal why organizations rise and fall, and how they can rise again in the face of change and adversity.

Choose to Win by Tom Ziglar
Most people don't get intentional about their lives until they face a crisis and are forced to make changes. This book reveals a plan for taking action *now*, for beating the status quo and building the life readers have dreamed about and deserve.

The Fun Formula by Joel Comm
Comm demonstrates that the best path to success – in work and in life – is to focus on our internal passions, curiosity, and the things that bring us great pleasure instead of the outside stuff we cannot change or control.

2 Chairs by Bob Beaudine
In 2 Chairs, Bob Beaudine offers three vital questions for working through trouble: Does God know your situation? Is it too hard for Him to handle? Does He have a good plan for you? Following these questions, Beaudine offers practical steps for readers to walk courageously, faithfully, and cheerfully through trouble—whether it is a minor issue or a major crisis.

Who Moved My Cheese? By Spencer Johnson
A simple parable that reveals profound truths about managing change. It is an amusing and enlightening story of four characters who live in a Maze and look for Cheese to nourish them and make them happy. This bestselling classic illustrates how to anticipate change, adapt quickly, and get ready to change and adapt again and again.

ABOUT THE AUTHOR

Michael Alan Tate is founder and president of On the Same Page Consulting, a management consulting firm that provides strategic facilitation for executive teams and career coaching for individuals facing significant work/life transitions. He is the author of *The White Shirt*, which is the first book in The White Shirt Series and is based on the simple principles and straightforward strategies that have worked for his clients for over 20 years. Mike is also the author of *Design a Life That Works*, a book for successful people who want to get their career, family, and faith on the same page. He writes a monthly blog, The Leadership and Life Journal, and hosts a podcast "Small-Time Leaders." Mike's website is www.michaelalantate.com.

Successful leaders facing significant changes rely on Michael Alan "Mike" Tate for handcrafted strategies to experience a healthy transition in their leadership and life. This author is also a podcaster, popular speaker and retreat facilitator on designing an On the Same Page Plan© for your career, your team or your organization in less time that you ever imagined.

As an executive coach, consultant and strategist for more than twenty years, Mike's experiences have made it clear that busy people want to make good decisions faster, have fun doing it, and see something happen sooner than later. As he often says, "A darn good plan today is better that a perfect plan six months from tomorrow."

Visit his websites to see some samples of his On the Same Page plans, learn about his unique consulting approach, and take a peak at his books: *Design a Life that Works*, *The White Shirt*, and *On the Same Page*. You can also sign up for his monthly newsletter the *Leadership and Life Journal* and listen to his podcast *Small-time Leaders* at:

www.michaelalantate.com

CPSIA information can be obtained
at www.ICGtesting.com
Printed in the USA
JSHW021743090620
6140JS00013B/73